Sue Cook's

Christmas

CROSS STITCH COLLECTION

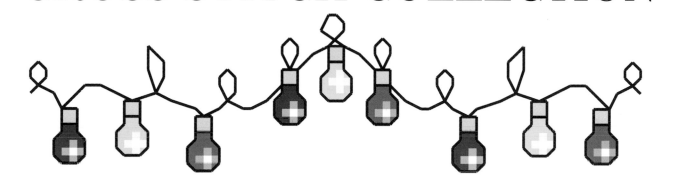

D&C

David and Charles

For my family, who make it all possible.

A DAVID & CHARLES BOOK

David & Charles is a subsidiary of F+W (UK) Ltd.,
an F+W Publications Inc. company

First published in the UK in 2005

Distributed in North America
by F+W Publications, Inc.
4700 East Galbraith Road
Cincinnati, OH 45236
1-800-289-0963

A catalogue record for this book is available from the British Library.

ISBN 0 7153 1912 4

Photography by Ginette Chapman and Karl Adamson

Printed in China by SNP Leefung
for David & Charles
Brunel House   Newton Abbot   Devon

EXECUTIVE EDITOR   Cheryl Brown
DESK EDITOR   Ame Verso
PROJECT EDITOR   Betsy Hosegood
ART EDITOR   Prudence Rogers

Visit our website at www.davidandcharles.co.uk

David & Charles books are available from all good bookshops; alternatively you can contact our
Orderline on (0)1626 334555 or write to us at FREEPOST EX2 110, David & Charles Direct,
Newton Abbot, TQ12 4ZZ (no stamp required UK mainland).

Contents

Introduction

As the days draw in and the nights grow ever longer, the run-up to Christmas is the perfect time to snuggle up indoors with a good embroidery project. With six fabulous themed pictures and over 100 quick-to-stitch motifs, this book is your ideal design source. It includes ideas on making cards (pages 12–13), Christmas-tree decorations (pages 24–27), a Christmas stocking (page 54), a tray cloth (page 82) and much more. These designs will enable you to make a variety of special presents as well as a wonderful collection of Christmas items for your own home. Remember, no matter how small or simple the project, a hand-stitched item is priceless in terms of the love that was put into it.

This book contains six chapters focusing on your favourite themes – Traditional Christmas, Victorian Christmas, Spirit of Christmas, Winter Wonderland, Santa and Friends, and Feast of Christmas. Each chapter begins with a cross stitch picture to set the scene and is followed by several smaller projects that would make ideal presents or quick-stitch items.

The charts for all the designs and others on the same theme follow. You can stitch these directly or combine them to make your own designs, as I did on a coaster (page 80).

A number of Christmas-style alphabets are also provided, conveniently assembled at the back of the book to enable you to personalize your work with a seasonal greeting or the recipient's name. Useful instructions on incorporating lettering into your designs are provided, and you'll also find details on adapting or personalizing your work in other exciting ways (see pages 7 and 98).

In the spirit of the season I have used beads and metallic threads as well as stranded embroidery cotton (floss) in some of my designs, and in places I've chosen to work on alternative materials such as the perforated silver paper used for the heart gift box (see page 68). I have included advice on working with all these options.

I feel that this book has brought me full circle, back to the small Christmas cards that I first started stitching. It has been a joy to work on and I hope this shines through on every page and that this book becomes a treasured part of your stitching library.

Christmas Inspirations

Christmas is definitely the season for creative cross stitch. Beautiful fabrics, shimmering threads, sparkly beads and festive buttons and charms can transform even the simplest design into something very special. In fact, if you have always wanted to add a new dimension to your stitching there are plenty of small motifs in this book for you to experiment with. Adding these touches will make your gifts and pictures unique, so consider my projects as a template for your own creativity and unleash the designer within.

Stitching Tips

Half stitches Many of the main picture charts use half cross stitches, but if you prefer, you can stitch the whole design in full cross stitch. Although your finished project will have a much denser look it will not detract from the picture. Make sure, though, that you follow the key in the same way as if you were using the different stitches. For more information on using the charts see Basic Techniques, page 98.

Saving remnants Some of the smaller designs need only tiny amounts of thread so save your leftovers. To prevent them getting tangled wind them onto a small piece of thin card and label with the shade number. Collect all your Christmas colours together before starting your project and you'll probably be surprised how many shades from the key you already have.

Fabrics and trimmings You can find fabrics and trimmings suitable for Christmas all year round, but look out for bargains just after the holiday when many items are reduced. Store them in a special festive 'scraps' box, which you can dip into for inspiration when you are ready to start your stitching. Delving into a pile of ribbons, fabrics, trimmings and charms is just the way to get creativity flowing.

Mixed media Take advantage of the many beautiful papers, stamps, pens and trimmings available by combining your stitching with stamps, stickers and so on. (See also Creative Card Making, page 12).

Bead bonanza Beads add sparkle to Christmas projects and some of the smaller designs in this book can be worked exclusively in them. They come in various shapes and sizes, but seed beads are the best size for cross stitch designs (see opposite). Look out for 'bead nabbers', which fit over your finger and have a surface designed to make picking up tiny beads less tedious.

Cross stitch borders Some of the pictures, such as Winter Wonderland, have borders made up of single lines of cross stitch. I find that it helps to keep the tension of these border stitches a little looser than usual. If they are too tight they will often pull out of shape when the embroidery is stretched ready for framing, making an unattractive crooked line. Once the mount and frame have been added the fault will become even more apparent.

Get Creative

Different techniques can change the look of a design significantly, and to give you an idea of the possibilities I have used the small star motif from Santa and Friends (page 70) to demonstrate some alternatives. Use this motif as a reference to inspire you to explore any of the designs in this book using these or other techniques or even combining them in your own way. Refer to Materials and Equipment, page 97, for advice on choosing fabric.

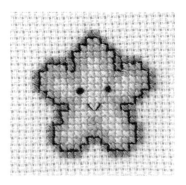

Standard technique Here the design is stitched in the conventional way on cream 14-count Aida using two strands for the cross stitch and one strand for the backstitch and French knots.

Enlargement To enlarge a design the easy way, work on a lower count fabric, such as 11-count Aida or on 22-count Hardanger, as shown, working over two fabric threads. I used three strands of thread for the cross stitch and two strands for the backstitch and French knots. This is perfect for baby projects.

Festive sparkle Work on a shiny fabric like the white/pearl lustre 14-count Aida shown here and introduce sparkly threads or braids. Here rayon threads were used for the cross stitch and a gold metallic braid for the star outline. The darker blue edging gives a sharper outline and makes the star appear brighter.

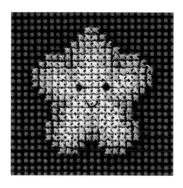

Perforated paper If you wish to cut your stitching out, as for the Tree Treasures on page 26, work on perforated paper or plastic. I used 14-count navy blue perforated paper here, stitching it in the conventional way. Use sharp scissors to cut out the motif, working close to the stitches.

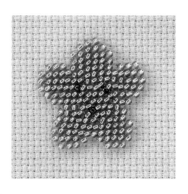

Beadwork Adding beads to cross stitch is an established technique favoured by the Victorians. Seed beads are easiest to use and decorate without dominating. Here the design was worked on pale blue 14-count Aida with gold beads used in place of the yellow thread and darker beads for the eyes and mouth. Both the blue edging and backstitch have been omitted. The rounded star on the soft background gives a delicate look.

Needlepoint canvas To show just how versatile these charts can be I stitched the star in yellow pearl cotton on 14-count needlepoint canvas. A solid blue square around the star worked in random-dyed pearl cotton adds a modern twist.

Traditional Christmas

Christmas is the time when many of us dig out our family traditions – the fairy that has always been on top of the tree, those lick-and-stick paper chains, and glass baubles that have been in the family as long as we can remember, as well as making our own greetings cards and decorations. At this time of year we are naturally drawn to nostalgic images of carol singers, Christmas crackers, robins, wreaths and Christmas stockings, as in this main design and on the cards, tags and chart pages that follow.

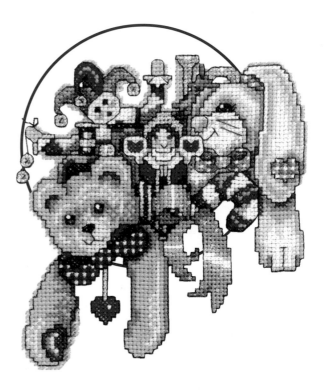

You will need

- Cream 14-count Aida 38 x 30cm (15 x 12in)
- DMC stranded cotton (floss) and metallic gold as listed in the key
- Tapestry needle size 26
- Mount board and picture frame of your choice

Design size: 24 x 15.3cm (9½ x 6in)
Stitch count: 133 high x 83 wide

1 Find and mark the centre of the fabric. Starting in the centre and following the chart on pages 10–11, begin by working the full cross stitch in two strands. Now work the half cross stitch in two strands. Where metallic thread is used combine one strand of the colour listed in the key with one strand of DMC gold thread.

2 Work all the backstitch and French knots in one strand of 838 or blanc.

3 When you have completed all the stitching, wash and press your work and prepare it for framing, following the instructions on page 102.

Opposite: Cream Aida is softer than white, complementing the thread colours and adding to the traditional feel. For a three-dimensional look, the stocking has grey half cross stitch shadows. Full cross stitch would have been too heavy, distracting from the main design. Gold thread reflects the sparkle of Christmas and will shimmer in the light.

Stocking

DMC stranded cotton

Full cross stitch
2 strands

	704	N 725	╱ 727	L 739	V 746	Z 754	■ 814	• 838	948	△ 3042	O 3746	T 3853	Y 3854	╲ 3855
• blanc	＜ 318	■ 333	⊥ 340	V 341	I 352	414	415	I 433	435	437	✳ 498	✖ 666	699	I 701

Full cross stitch
1 strand cotton +
1 strand metallic gold

725 + gold	727 + gold	783 + gold

Half cross stitch
2 strands cotton

3041	3042

Backstitch
1 strand
— 838

French knots
○ blanc
● 838

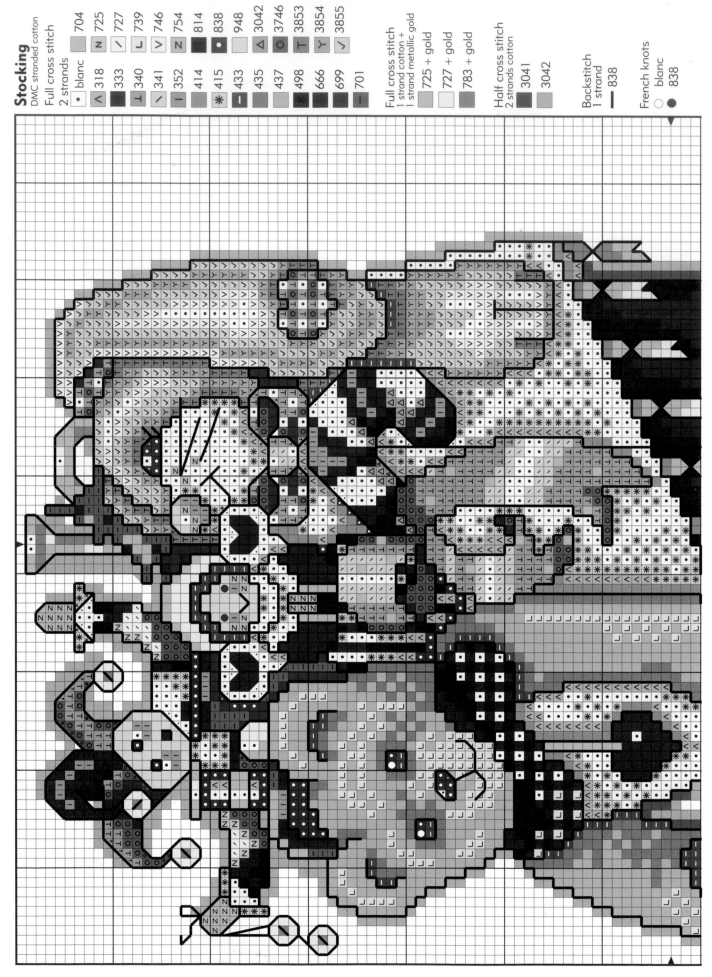

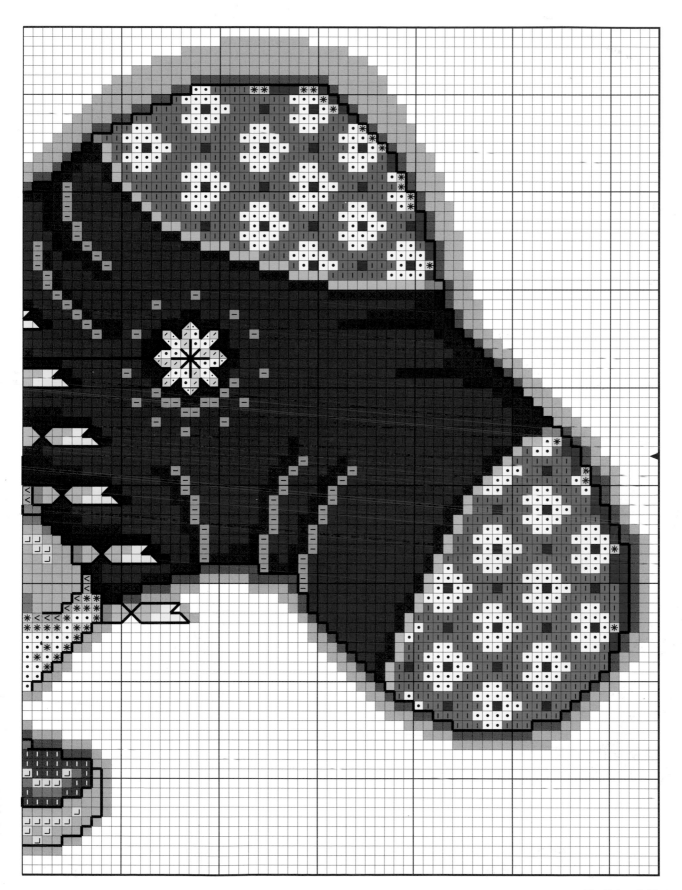

Creative Card Making

Many of the small designs in this book are ideal for card making, being perfectly sized and quick to stitch. This is a good opportunity to experiment with alternative techniques, utilizing beads or sparkling threads or stitching on perforated paper or plastic canvas. Consider your choices of aperture or standard card blanks and add co-ordinating papers, stickers, charms, buttons and so on in festive colours to produce lovely unique cards in no time.

Co-ordinated trimmings are key to successful card making. Here the angel's wand is echoed by the star stickers and the colour of the padded fabric hearts, while on the heart tag the same colour is used for the tie as for the cross stitch. The angel was stitched on pearl lustre 14-count Aida, treated afterwards with PVA glue (see page 98), and then cut out when dry. See page 18 for the angel and heart designs.

Making Cards

This card uses an aperture card blank in a new way. Instead of being placed within the aperture, the cross stitch design graces the front. I worked this topiary design (from page 15) on fabric and stiffened it with PVA glue (see page 98), then cut it out and stuck it in place. Behind the aperture the curtain is red felt patterned with gold dots, which I cut to shape and edged with lace. Fine gold ribbon creates the tieback effect and a gold metallic paper suggests the light from the room beyond.

Using aperture cards

You can buy ready-made aperture cards like the one used for the card below with many attractive cut-outs including windows, stars and Christmas trees as well as more conventional circles and squares. These need careful planning to ensure that they work successfully. They come in limited sizes and shapes so you need to choose the card first and then select a design that sits nicely inside the aperture. Ideally place your fabric behind the opening and count the visible squares to see what will fit. Alternatively, invest in a decent aperture cutter, available from scrapbooking suppliers, and make your own cards with apertures to fit your favourite designs.

Using plain cards

Cross stitched fabric can be applied to standard card blanks or to cards you have made yourself from card stock. One method is to work the stitching on perforated card or plastic and trim it around the stitching, then simply glue in place on the card front. Alternatively, work on Aida or evenweave fabric and apply PVA glue to stiffen the design so you can cut it out, as I did on the angel card shown opposite. You can even trim the fabric to a square or rectangle and fray the edges to provide a neat finish before sticking in place. Apply lightweight iron-on interfacing to the back of your fabric to give your stitching a smooth look.

Co-ordinating the details

The best way to ensure a successful result is to do all the shopping for your card in one hit, buying fabric, threads, card and embellishments at the same time. Alternatively, if you have already stitched your motif or have paper or stickers that you want to use, take these with you when you buy the other items.

Utilizing specialist papers

Specialist papers can make or break a card. Holographic and metallic papers are often self-adhesive and can provide the ideal Christmas sparkle. Handmade papers work well too, such as the mulberry paper used to make the cloud behind the angel on the card opposite. By wetting it with a little water on a soft brush you can tear it for a feathered look.

Christmas Greenery

DMC stranded cotton

Cross stitch

• blanc	I 341	╱ 436	T 783	3746		**French knots**
╲ 165	349	437	815			● 310
310	351	725	905			
318	L 415	O 727	906		**Backstitch**	**Beads**
340	434	+ 745	— 907		— 310	◎ yellow
					— 838	

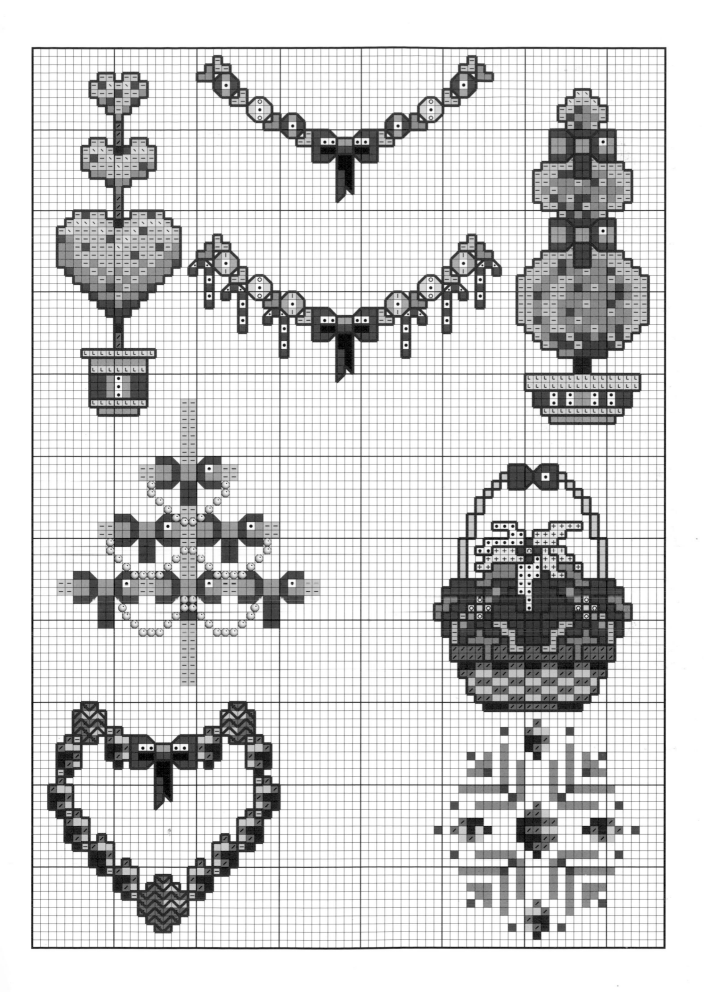

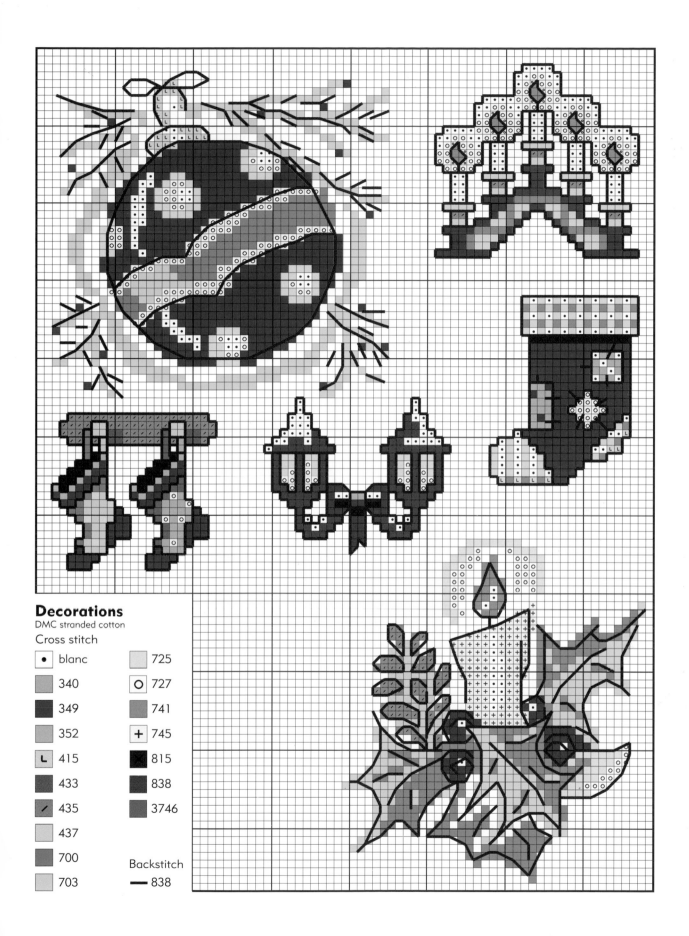

Decorations
DMC stranded cotton

Cross stitch

•	blanc		725
	340	O	727
	349		741
	352	+	745
L	415	✕	815
	433		838
╱	435		3746
	437		
	700	**Backstitch**	
	703	▬	838

Christmas Wishes

Baaa......

Humbug!

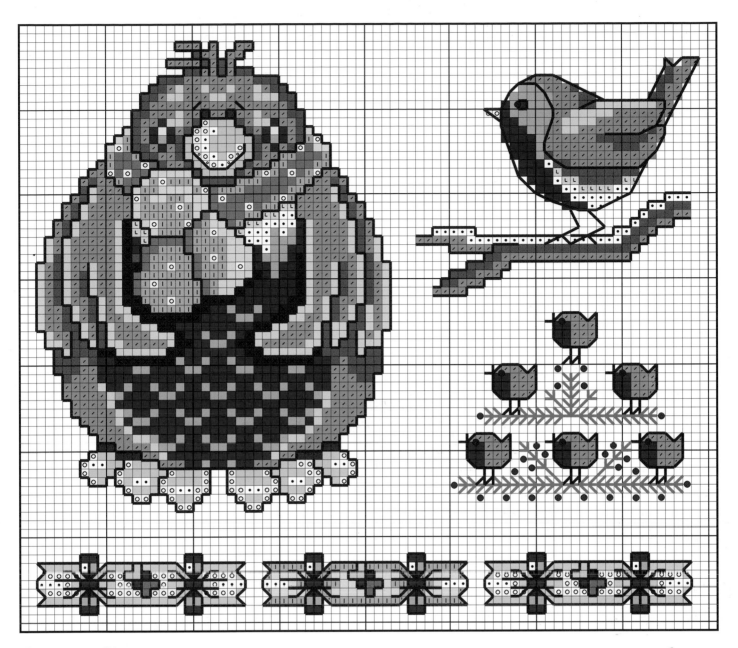

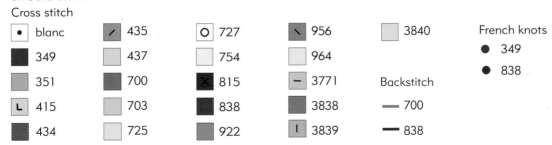

Christmas Characters

DMC stranded cotton

Cross stitch

• blanc	╱ 435	O 727	╲ 956	3840
■ 349	437	754	964	
351	700	✗ 815	— 3771	
L 415	703	838	3838	
434	725	922	I 3839	

French knots

● 349

● 838

Backstitch

— 700

— 838

Victorian Christmas

Prince Albert is credited with introducing the fashion of decorated fir trees to the Royal Household in the 1850s. The idea soon caught on, appealing to the Victorians' lavish sense of style, and now it is an almost universal tradition, forming the centrepiece of our festive decorations. Traditionally trees would have been lit with candles, as in the picture here, and decorated with sweets, baubles and handmade decorations like the ones on the following pages.

You will need

- Cream 14-count Aida 38 x 36cm (15 x 14in)
- DMC stranded cotton (floss) including two skeins of green (3346) and metallic gold as listed in key
- Seed beads in red and gold
- Approximately 12 tiny gold star charms (optional)
- Tapestry needle size 26
- Mount board and picture frame of your choice

Design size: 24 x 20cm (9½ x 8in)
Stitch count: 133 high x 111 wide

1 Find and mark the centre of the fabric. Starting in the centre and following the chart on pages 22–23, begin by working the full cross stitch in two strands. Now work the half cross stitch in two strands. Where metallic thread is used combine one strand of the colour listed in the key with one strand of DMC gold thread.

2 Work all the backstitch in one strand of 838. Then work the backstitch in one strand of yellow (725) and one strand of DMC metallic gold thread.

3 Add the beads where shown on the chart, following the instructions on page 101. I've scattered tiny gold star charms in the tree branches to catch the light but this is optional.

4 When you have completed all the stitching, wash and press your work and prepare it for framing, following the instructions on page 102.

Opposite: I've used several shades of one colour to give the effect of the folds in the rich curtain fabric and the glow of the candlelight on the tree. You may find it useful to thread up separate needles to stitch these areas.

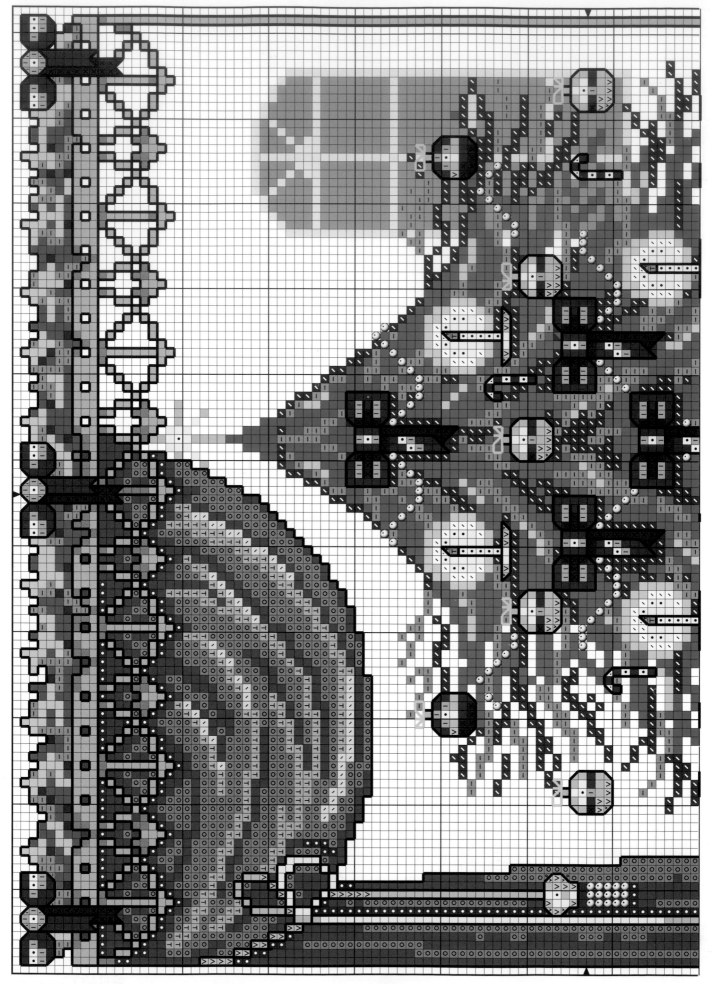

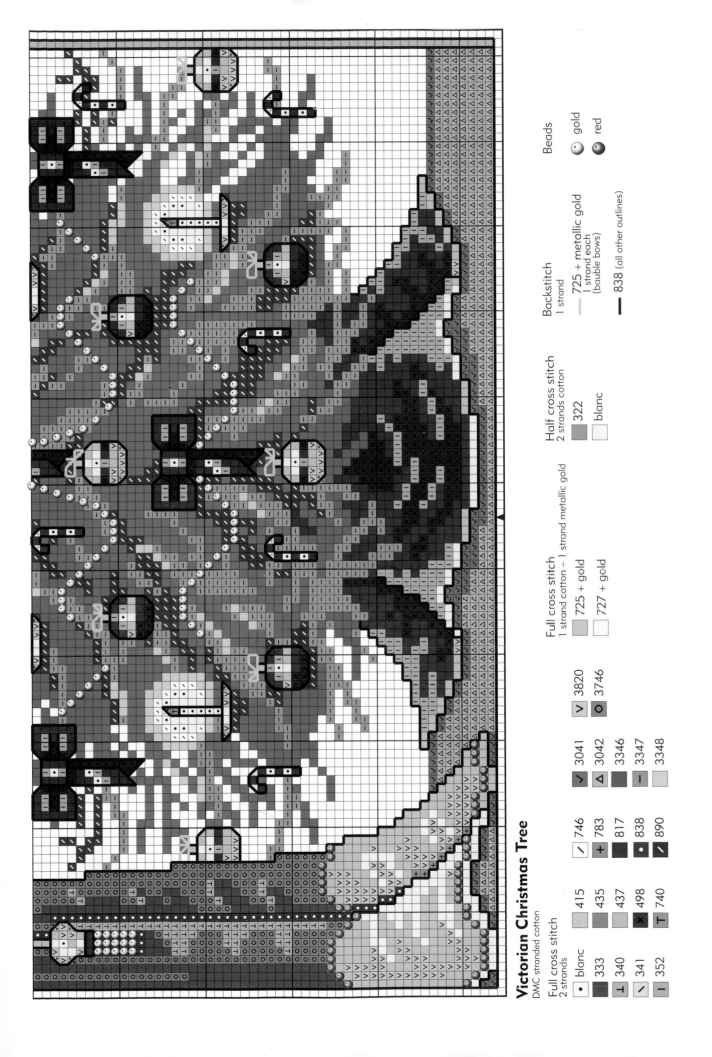

Victorian Christmas Tree

DMC stranded cotton

Full cross stitch
2 strands

•	blanc	/	746
	415	+	783
	333	✕	817
⊤	340	●	838
/	341	—	838
I	352	/	890

	415		
	435		
	437		
✕	498		
⊤	740		

✓	3820	✓	3041
○	3746	△	3042
			3346
		—	3347
			3348

Full cross stitch
1 strand cotton – 1 strand metallic gold

	725 + gold
	727 + gold

Half cross stitch
2 strands cotton

	322
	blanc

Backstitch
1 strand

— 725 + metallic gold
1 strand each
(bauble bows)

— 838 (all other outlines)

Beads

◉ gold
◐ red

Elegant Tree Decorations

Recapture the excitement of Christmases past with this angel and coordinating tree hangings. The angelic tree topper is every little girl's dream, with her golden hair and sumptuous fabric skirt. The tasselled ornament echoes the hand-stitched cushions so popular with the Victorians, while the dainty boot emulates their love of traditional découpage designs.

Opposite: The angel's skirt can be made from any firm fabric, plain or self-patterned, provided it isn't too thick to gather. Once the cross stitched angel has been stiffened with glue, she can be cut out without fraying and attached to the fabric skirt.

These tree hangings reflect the Victorians' love of richly coloured handicrafts and decoration. The simple motifs have been embellished with gold beads and trimmed with pretty tassels and lace. I stitched the tasselled ornament on perforated plastic, but you can use paper, if preferred.

Tree Treasures

You will need

DAINTY BOOT
- Cream perforated paper 12 x 9cm (4½ x 3½in)
- 5cm (2in) of 6mm (¼in) narrow lace (optional)

TASSELLED ORNAMENT
- Brown perforated plastic 10 x 10cm (4 x 4in)
- Stranded cotton (floss) for tassels

FOR EACH DECORATION
- DMC stranded cotton (floss) as listed in the key
- Gold and other coloured beads (optional)
- Gold card for backing a little larger than each design
- Tapestry needle size 26
- Beading needle size 10 or sharp embroidery needle (optional)
- 15cm (6in) of 6mm (¼in) gold ribbon for each hanging
- Clear glue
- Scissors

1 Use a ruler to find the centre of the perforated paper or plastic and mark with a pencil dot. Starting in the centre and following the chart on page 29, begin by working the full cross stitch in two strands. For the boot I replaced 725 in the key with tiny gold beads for buttons; for the ornament I also used gold beads and replaced some of the other colours in the chart with beads of a similar colour. If using beads refer to the general instructions on page 101 for helpful hints.

2 Work the backstitch in one strand of 838. It is not necessary to do this if you have beaded any of the areas of backstitch on the chart.

3 For the ornament only, use three stands of 777 to complete the backstitch as shown on the chart. Make up the tassels as explained on page 99 or purchase some ready-made. Refer to the photograph for placement and stitch them securely in place.

4 Use sharp scissors to cut carefully around the outline of the design as close to the stitching as possible. Attach a lace trim to the boot, if desired, using a little clear glue and referring to the picture for positioning. Fold the ends to the back and secure with a dot of glue.

5 Fold the gold ribbon in half to form a hanger and glue the ends together. Glue the ribbon centrally to the top back of the design and leave to dry.

6 Spread clear glue thinly over the back of the stitched piece and, when this is tacky, glue to the gold card with wrong sides together; leave to dry. Now carefully trim away the excess card, taking care not to snip the ribbon hanger or the tassels of the ornament.

'Tis the season...

...to give a loved one a special gift
Stitch a set of tree hangings, wrap them in tissue paper and put them in a pretty box as a gift for someone you love. Personalize the gift by working the designs in the recipient's favourite colours.

Angel Tree Topper

1 Find and mark the centre of the evenweave fabric. Starting in the centre and following the chart on page 29, work the cross stitch in two strands over two threads of fabric.

2 Work all the backstitch and French knots in one strand of 838.

3 Stiffen the stitched piece with PVA glue, following the instructions on page 98. Once the glue is dry, cut out the angel with sharp scissors, following the line of the stitching as closely as possible.

4 Lay the angel onto the gold card with wrong sides facing and draw around the outline with a pencil. Cut out the gold card.

5 Sew the lace to the bottom long edge of the co-ordinating fabric, taking a 6mm (¼in) seam allowance. Lightly press. Lay tulle (net) on the wrong side of the fabric. Fold both layers together with the right sides of the fabric facing and stitch the short side seam with a 6mm (¼in) seam allowance. You now have a tube.

6 Use neat running stitch to gather the top edge as tightly as possible, so it is no more than 5cm (2in) wide. Arrange the skirt into a bell shape.

7 Using clear glue, attach the skirt to the wrong side of the angel, approximately 5cm (2in) above the bottom edge of her bodice. When completely dry, use clear glue to stick the gold card to the back of the angel, covering the gathered edge of the skirt (see the photograph on page 99). Pinch and hold together the pieces around the top of the skirt to ensure they are stuck securely.

A delicate gold lace trim adds the final touch to the angel's skirt and will glint and gleam under the Christmas lights.

'Tis the season…

…to use your creative flair

The finished angel will look spectacular on top of your Christmas tree but if you prefer you can slide her over a glass or cardboard tube and stand her on a table or shelf.

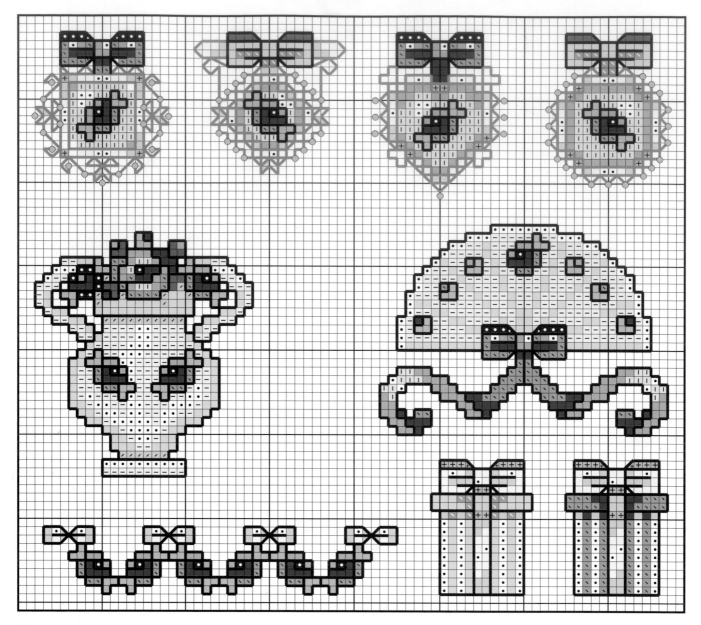

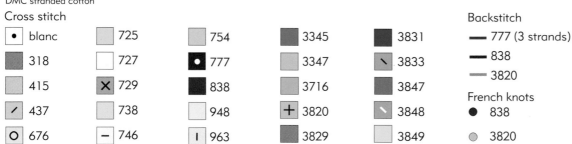

Victorian Flair

DMC stranded cotton

Cross stitch

• blanc	725	754	3345	3831
318	727	777	3347	3833
415	✗ 729	838	3716	3847
╱ 437	738	948	+ 3820	3848
O 676	— 746	‖ 963	3829	3849

Backstitch

— 777 (3 strands)

— 838

— 3820

French knots

● 838

○ 3820

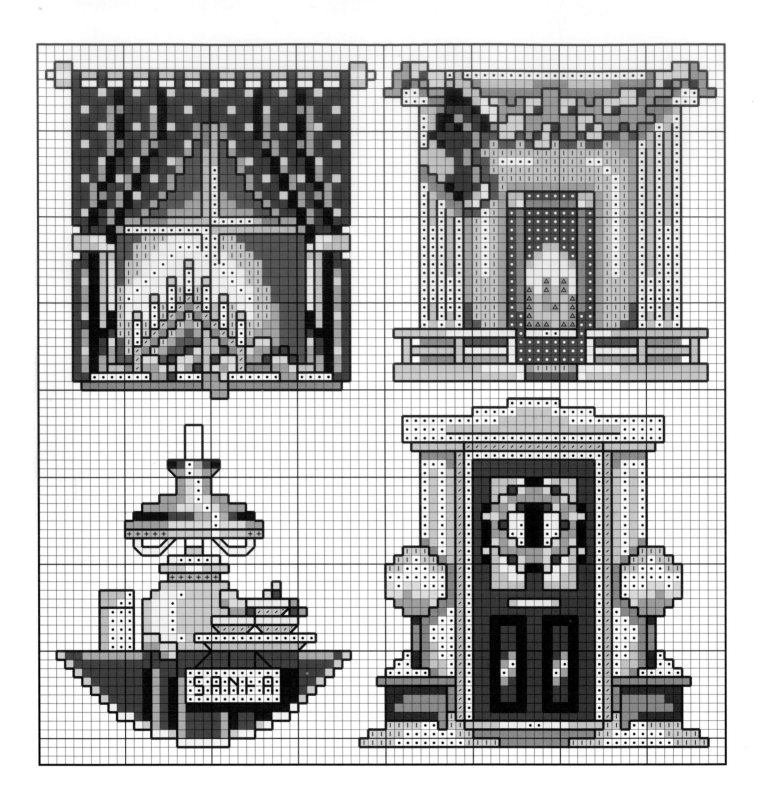

Warm Welcome
DMC stranded cotton

Cross stitch

• blanc	I 341	434
⊙ 317	349	435
318	352	╱ 437
340	415	712

725	815	3348
727	838	3746
O 739	— 3345	3747
△ 740	3347	+ 3820

Backstitch

— 838

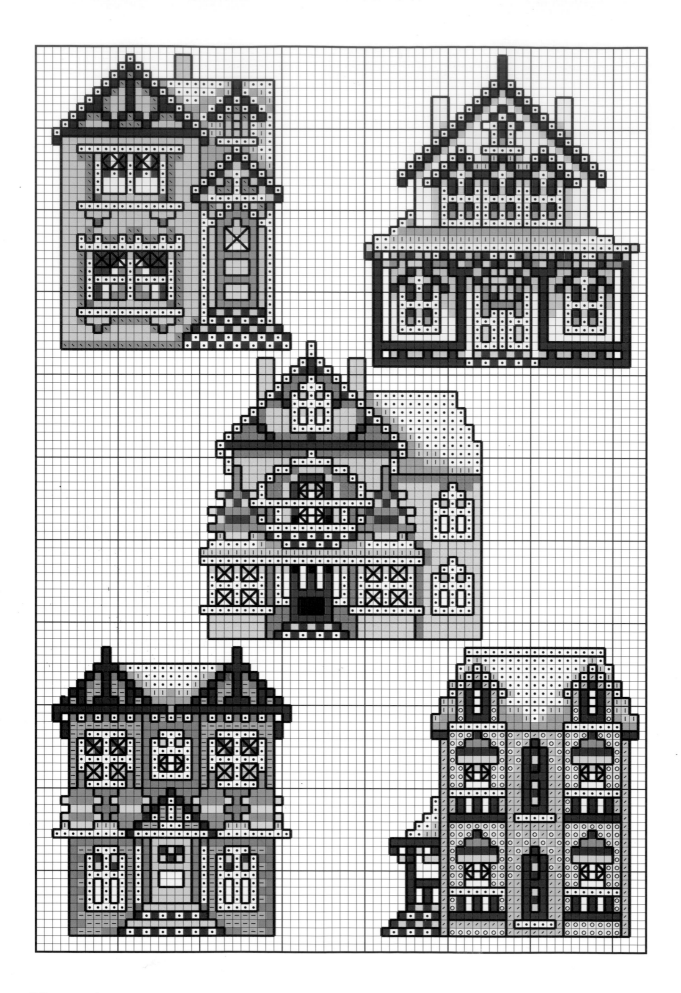

House and Home
DMC stranded cotton

Cross stitch

• blanc	349	\ 553	838	Backstitch
316	351	554	3347	— 838
318	415	725	3348	French knots
340	/ 437	727	— 3727	● 349
I 341	498	O 739		

Spirit of Christmas

In the hectic rush of preparing for the festivities it is all too easy to forget the true meaning of Christmas. But the simple story of this miraculous birth never loses its powerful appeal, and for generations children have retold it in their school plays. This stunning nativity scene is framed by a rich gold border in medieval style, and the deep blue stillness of the night contrasts with the glow from the manger and bright robes of the angels. The wise men feature separately on a bell pull and additional cherubs adorn two scented sachets that accompany this picture.

You will need

- Cream 14-count Aida 38 x 36cm (15 x 14in)
- DMC stranded cotton (floss) including two skeins of indigo (823) and metallic gold as listed in the key
- Tapestry needle size 26
- Mount board and picture frame of your choice

Design size: 23.6 x 20cm (9¼ x 8in)
Stitch count: 130 high x 110 wide

1 Find and mark the centre of the fabric. Starting in the centre and following the chart on pages 36–37, begin by working the full cross stitch in two strands. Now work the half cross stitch in two strands. Where metallic thread is used combine one strand of the colour listed in the key with one strand of DMC gold thread.

2 Work all the backstitch in one strand of the colours listed in the key apart from the metallic areas. Then work the backstitch in one strand of yellow (725) and one strand of DMC metallic thread.

3 When you have completed all the stitching, wash and press your work and prepare it for framing, following the instructions on page 102.

Opposite: Although this picture is very densely stitched, much of the background is made up of half cross stitch. As well as adding depth to the design, this allows large areas to grow quite quickly. An alternative is to use a blue fabric for the background, stitching only the colours of the sunset, but if you do this choose your fabric carefully. If possible, take some of the threads with you when you go to buy the fabric because the wrong colour combination could spoil the effect of your stitching.

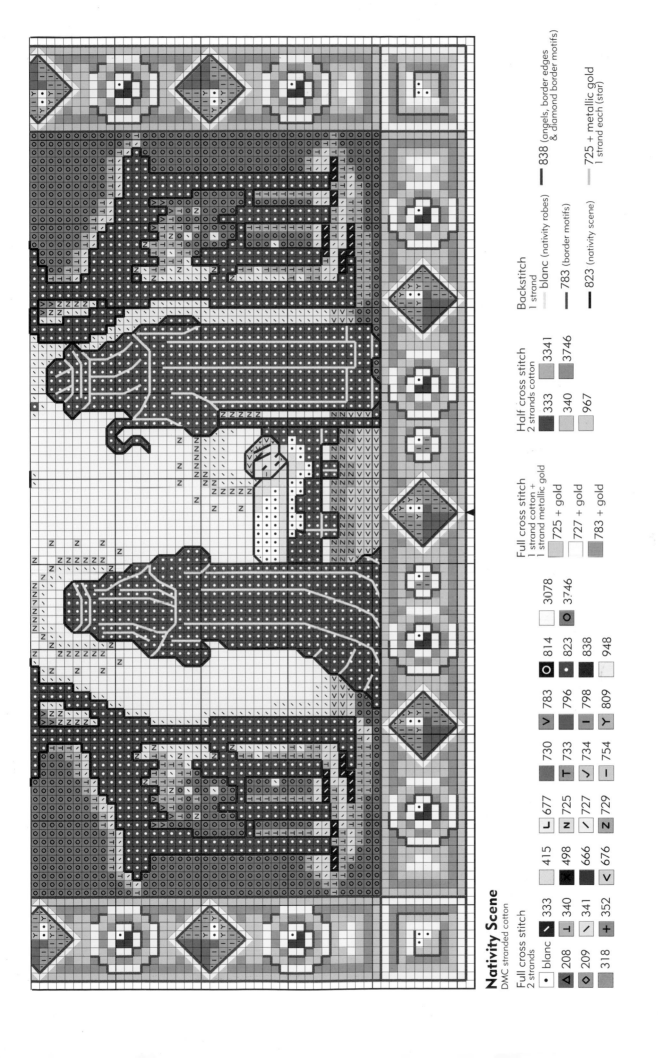

Nativity Scene

DMC stranded cotton

Full cross stitch
2 strands

•	blanc	L	677	
◢	208	N	725	
◇	209	✓	727	
	318	Z	729	
+	352	✓	676	

/	333	T	730	
⊥	340	T	733	
✗	341	✓	734	
/	415	—	754	
✗	498			
	666			

	3078		
⊙	814	V	783
●	823	V	796
	838	I	798
	948	Y	809

Full cross stitch
1 strand cotton +
1 strand metallic gold

	725 + gold
	727 + gold
	783 + gold

Half cross stitch
2 strands cotton

	333		3341
	340		3746
	967		

Backstitch
1 strand

— blanc (nativity robes)
— 783 (border motifs)
— 823 (nativity scene)
— 838 (angels, border edges & diamond border motifs)
— 725 + metallic gold 1 strand each (star)

Festive Tree and Wall Hangings

Hanging decorations are a must at Christmas, not only on the tree but also on doors, walls, windows and any other flat surface that is in need of some Christmas spirit. This festive bell pull, featuring the Three Wise Men, will definitely be on display year after year, while the angel sachets would make wonderful presents or could be displayed on beds, chairs or sofas.

This cheerful girl angel is kindly bringing a decoration to the festivities. She graces a sachet that can be filled with potpourri or dried flowers. Look out for potpourri mixtures with spicy Christmas scents that are available in the run up to the big day. Another sachet is shown on page 40.

Opposite: These Three Wise Men are all basically worked from one design, although the star only moves into view behind the final figure. I have used festive colours for their clothing and saddlecloths, but you can use any colours. The blue felt of the backing makes a smart background and is easy to work with.

Scented Sachets

You will need

LOVE ANGEL SACHET

- Antique beige 14-count Aida 14cm (5½in) square
- Contrasting fabric 14cm (5½in) square for backing
- 60cm (24in) of 6mm (¼in) twisted red and gold cord
- Small red and green tartan fabric star (optional)

JOY ANGEL SACHET

- Cream/gold Lurex thread 14-count Aida 13cm (5¼in) square
- Contrasting fabric 13cm (5¼in) square for backing
- 56cm (22in) of 6mm (¼in) twisted cream and gold cord
- Three small red fabric hearts (optional)

FOR EACH SACHET

- DMC stranded cotton (floss) as listed in the key
- Tapestry needle size 26
- Small amount of filling
- Small amount of potpourri
- Clear glue or mini glue dots
- Sewing machine or usual sewing equipment

1 Find and mark the centre of the Aida. Starting in the centre and following the chart on page 47, work the cross stitch for your angel in two strands of embroidery cotton.

2 Work all the backstitch in one strand of the colours shown in the chart.

3 With right sides facing, pin the stitched piece to the backing fabric. Stitch together all round, taking a 12mm (½in) seam and leaving an opening at the bottom. Clip the seam allowance at the corners, turn the sachet out and press. Stuff firmly with wadding and push a small amount of potpourri into the centre. Do not close the opening yet.

4 Neatly stitch the twisted cord to the edges of the sachet, making a small loop at each corner as shown in the photographs. Use the opening at the lower edge to conceal the ends of the cord and then slipstitch closed.

5 If desired, attach the fabric star or the hearts with a spot of clear glue or use mini glue dots.

✫ 'Tis the season...

... for improvising

If you are working out of season appropriate potpourri may not be available. In this case you could fill the sachets with dried flowers such as camomile and hops for a sleep cushion or use some dried whole spices such as star anise, cloves and cinnamon sticks for a spicy Christmas scent. You can also change the motifs, choosing any you like.

Bell Pull

You will need

- Antique cream 14-count Aida 12.5 x 35cm (5 x 14in)
- DMC stranded cotton (floss) as listed in the key
- Tapestry needle size 26
- Two pieces of royal blue felt 12 x 42cm (4¾ x 16¾in)
- Piece of iron-on interfacing 7 x 30cm (3 x 12in)
- Three tassels or stranded cotton to make your own (see page 99)
- Gold star charm (optional)
- Pencil
- Ruler
- Sharp dressmaking scissors
- Plastic ring for hanging
- Sewing machine or usual sewing equipment

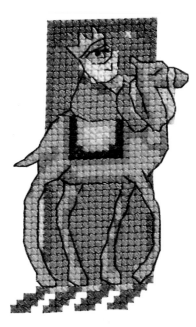

This design was stitched entirely in stranded cotton (floss), but you could use beads to draw attention to certain details, such as the guiding star, or use gold threads on their crowns for added shimmer.

1 Find and mark the centre of the Aida. Starting in the centre and following the chart on page 44, stitch the Three Wise Men vertically, leaving a space of two squares between each motif. Work the cross stitch in two strands.

2 Work all the backstitch and French knots in one strand of 310.

3 On the wrong side of the stitched piece use a ruler to measure 1cm (½in) each side of the widest points of your motifs and lightly mark with a pencil line.

4 Repeat for the top and bottom edge of the design but this time measuring 2.5cm (1in) away from the design. This is your stitching line. Now measure and mark 1cm (½in) beyond this to give your cutting line. Trim away the excess fabric.

5 Iron interfacing to the wrong side of the stitched piece. Turn the edges of the fabric to the wrong side and press firmly.

6 Measure 2.5cm (1in) from the top of one of the pieces of felt. Centre your stitched piece on the felt, placing the top edge level with your measured line. Pin the embroidery in place and stitch to the felt.

7 Use a ruler to mark a point at the lower end of the felt. You may wish to make a paper template first. Pin the two pieces of felt together and cut the point. Use dressmaking scissors with long blades to ensure you get a good straight line when cutting the felt.

8 Join the felt by topstitching the two pieces together 6mm (¼in) from the edges. Referring to the photograph on page 39 for placement, attach the three tassels to the points of the felt. Attach the star charm, if desired, and sew a small plastic ring to the back for hanging.

Peace and Joy
DMC stranded cotton

Cross stitch

• blanc	O 415	— 746	3041	I 3848	Backstitch	
310	420	\ 754	3042	3849	— 310	
340	/ 422	783	X 3743			
341	+ 725	817	3746		French knots	
351	727	948	3847		● 310	

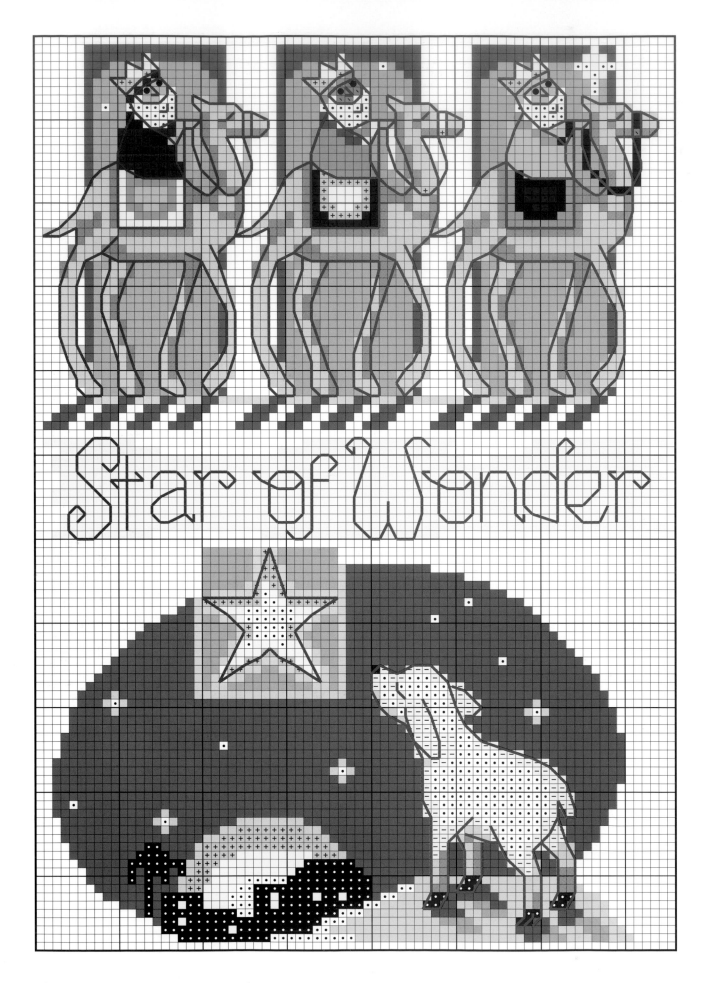

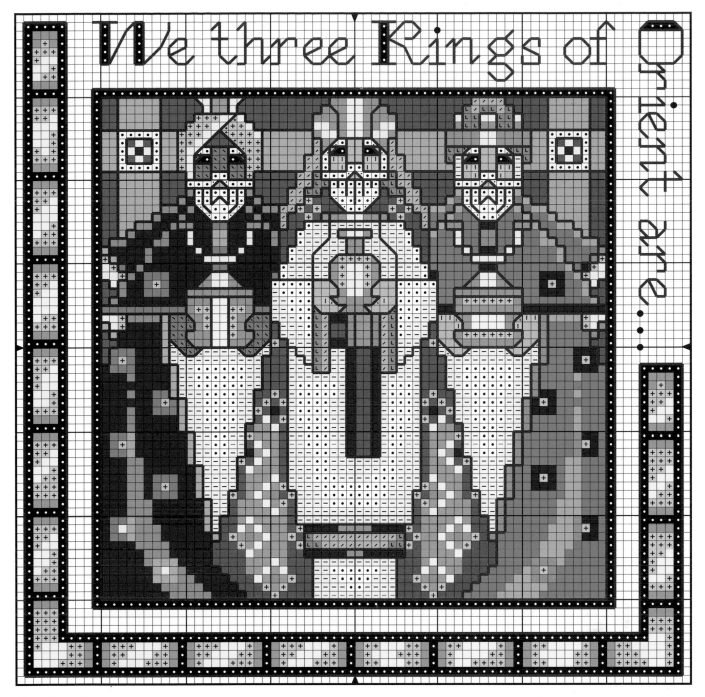

Guiding Star

DMC stranded cotton

Cross stitch

• blanc	╲ 407	+ 725	783	992
310	553	727	★ 815	I 3064
340	554	L 732	817	3746
341	612	╱ 734	950	
352	613	— 745	991	

Backstitch

— 310

French knots

● 310

A Host of Angels
DMC stranded cotton

Cross stitch

• blanc		
340	I 597	700
350	− 598	703
352	╱ 676	+ 725
453	L 677	727
	680	729

747	948
╲ 754	3808
O 758	3810
✕ 816	3861
838	

Backstitch
— 350
— 838

French knots
● 758
● 838

Winter Wonderland

To a child there is nothing quite like waking up to find an overnight fall of snow has magically transformed the landscape. Sledges are dug out and warm clothes hurriedly put on in the race to get outdoors. This main design captures all the pleasure of playing in the snow. As the sun sets in a fiery glow over the hills the snowmen have come to life in their winter wonderland. But if the weather keeps you indoors you can settle down with your cross stitch. You'll find plenty of motifs in this section to warm your heart.

You will need

- Pale apricot 28-count evenweave fabric 38 x 36cm (15 x 14in)
- DMC stranded cotton (floss) including two skeins of white cotton and white rayon thread as listed in the key
- Tapestry needle size 26
- Mount board and picture frame of your choice

Design size: 23.6 x 21cm (9¼ x 8¼in)
Stitch count: 130 high x 114 wide

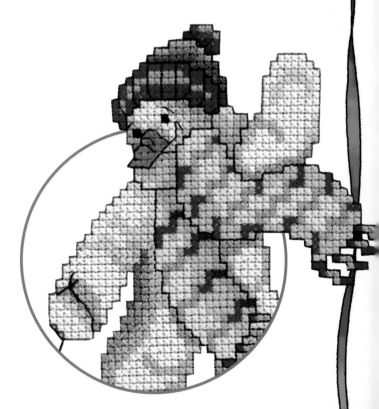

1 Find and mark the centre of the evenweave fabric. Starting in the centre and following the chart on pages 50–51, begin by working the full cross stitch in two strands over two threads of the fabric. Now work the half cross stitch in two strands. Where rayon thread is used combine one strand of white cotton with one strand of rayon thread.

2 Work all the backstitch and French knots in one strand of the colours listed in the key.

3 When you have completed all the stitching, wash and press your work and prepare it for framing, following the instructions on page 102.

Opposite: This design was worked on pale apricot fabric to re-create the glow of a winter sunset. It also works well with the blue and violet shadows in the snow. If you can't find a suitable apricot you could use pale blue. Avoid working on white fabric because you will lose the effect of the shimmer on the snowy fields created by the combination of white cotton and rayon thread.

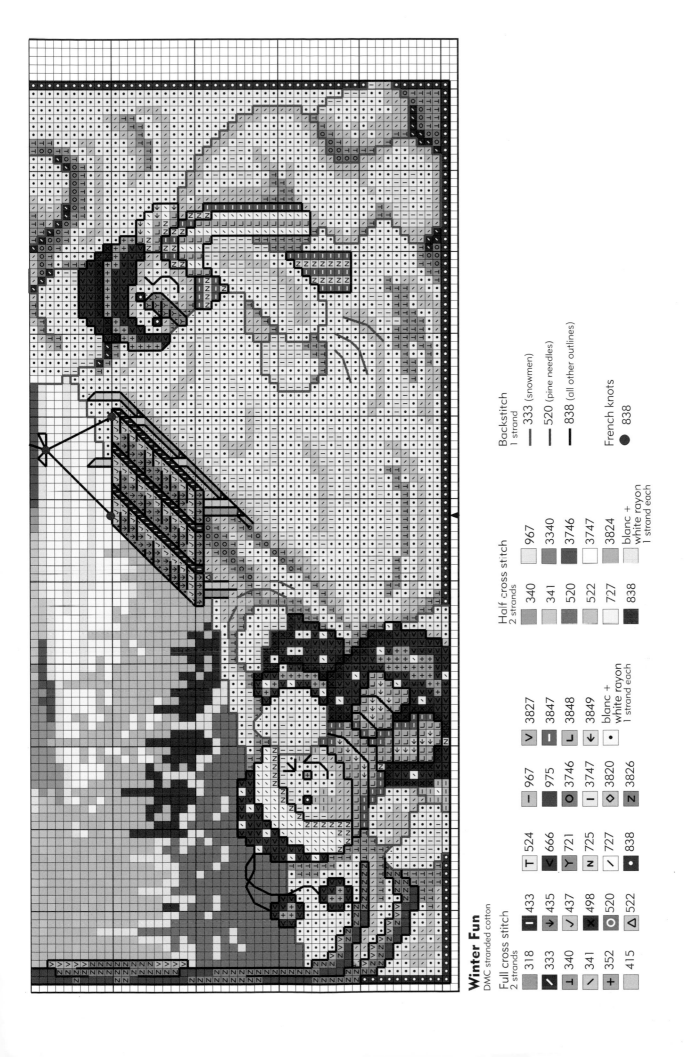

Winter Fun
DMC stranded cotton

Full cross stitch
2 strands

318	T 524	I 967	V 3827
333	V 666	975	I 3847
340	Y 721	O 3746	L 3848
341	N 725	I 3747	↓ 3849
X 498	/ 727	◇ 3820	• blanc + white rayon 1 strand each
+ 352	520	• 838	
415	Δ 522	Z 3826	

Half cross stitch
2 strands

340	967
341	3340
520	3746
522	3747
727	3824
838	blanc + white rayon 1 strand each

Backstitch
1 strand

— 333 (snowmen)
— 520 (pine needles)
— 838 (all other outlines)

French knots
● 838

Family Fun

On the night before Christmas children sometimes start to worry that Santa will overlook them or that they haven't been good enough for him to call. A bold sign, hung on the front door or your child's room door, will help catch his attention, while a stocking is an essential place for him to deposit gifts.

At just 12cm (4¾in) wide, this stocking could be hung on the tree or mantelpiece for Santa to fill or stuffed with sweets or a small gift that can be opened at the due time.

'Tis the season...

... for personalizing your gifts

Use an Aida band for the cuff of your Christmas stocking so that you can embroider your child's name on it. Use one of the alphabets on pages 91–96 to work the name, referring to the hints and guidelines on page 90 to help with positioning. Quick to stitch, you could make one of these for every member of the family.

Opposite: Even at the end of a long night delivering presents, Santa surely won't be able to resist coming to the home that has this sign to catch his attention. The stitching is mounted on felt-covered card with some ready-made gold card stars and stickers to glint and glimmer in the light.

Christmas Stocking

- Cream 14-count Aida 8 x 10cm (3⅛ x 4in)
- DMC stranded cotton (floss) as listed in the key
- Two pieces of blue felt 15 x 23cm (6 x 9in) – I used some printed with tiny silver dots
- Two pieces of white felt 6 x 14cm (2¼ x 5½in) – mine was printed with larger dots
- Three shiny red fabric stars (optional)
- 15cm (6in) of 2.5cm (1in) wide ribbon for hanging
- Graph paper and pencil
- Clear glue
- Sharp scissors
- Sewing machine or usual sewing equipment

1 Find and mark the centre of the Aida fabric. Starting in the centre and following the chart on page 59, work the cross stitch in two strands.

2 Work all the backstitch and French knots in one strand of 838. Now add a border of cross stitch in red (349), leaving a space of two squares all round the motif.

3 Use sharp scissors to cut out the design two or three squares beyond the stitched border and fray the fabric up to the stitching line.

4 Using a piece of graph paper the same size as the blue felt, draw a simple Christmas stocking shape. My stocking measures 12cm (4¾in) wide at the top and is 23cm (9in) long at the toe. Once you are happy with your template cut out the stocking and pin it to the felt. Cut two stockings from felt.

5 Pin the felt stockings together with wrong sides facing and topstitch together all round 6mm (¼in) from the edge.

6 Using all six strands of red (349), blanket stitch around the edge of the stocking, following the line of topstitching. You may find you need a very sharp embroidery needle to pierce the felt.

7 Spread a small amount of clear glue along the top edge of the stocking and approximately 6cm (2¼in) down the edges. Line up a piece of the white felt with the top of the stocking and position it centrally. You should have a slight overlap for a cuff effect. Press firmly into position. Repeat for the back of the stocking then glue the sides of the cuff together. There is no need to glue the lower edge of the cuff to the stocking. Add the three red stars using a spot of clear glue or mini glue dots.

8 Use a small amount of clear glue to stick the stitched patch onto the stocking at a slight angle. Finish by attaching the ribbon hanging, catching it into place with a few small stitches.

This Eskimo girl is happy no matter how cold it gets in her fur-lined coat, hat and boots. If you are making the stocking for a boy, you may prefer to use one of the penguins from page 57 or any of the other small designs.

Santa Stop Sign

You will need

- Cream 14-count Aida 19 x 20cm (7½ x 8in)
- DMC stranded cotton (floss) as listed in the key
- Tapestry needle size 26
- Mount board or firm card 14 x 16cm (5½ x 6¼in)
- Mount board or firm card 23 x 28cm (9 x 11in)
- Self-adhesive red felt 23 x 28cm (9 x 11in) or ordinary felt, which can be attached with double-sided tape
- Wadding (batting) 14 x 16cm (5½ x 6¼in)
- Four 7cm (2¾in) die-cut, gold corrugated card stars
- Four small red lurex stars
- Four gold holographic stars from a sheet of laser-cut stickers
- 38cm (15in) length of 15mm (⅝in) gold Lurex ribbon
- Foam sticky pads
- Double-sided tape
- Clear glue, pencil, ruler and scissors

1 Find and mark the centre of the Aida. Starting in the centre and following the chart on page 61, work the cross stitch in two strands.

2 Work all the backstitch and French knots in one strand of 838.

3 On the wrong side of the stitched piece, count ten squares beyond the widest points of the design and mark with a soft pencil line. Now count a further 12 squares beyond this and mark with another pencil line. This is your cutting line.

4 Cover the smaller piece of card with double-sided tape and press the wadding (batting) firmly into place. Place this card with the wadding against the wrong side of the stitched piece. Use the inner pencil line to help you position it centrally over the stitching.

5 Use double-sided tape to stick the stitched piece to the card. Stick the tape to the long edges of the card and fold the Aida over to the back. Start in the centre and pull the fabric gently to the back of the card, checking to see that the stitching is lying straight. When you are happy with the positioning, press down firmly and repeat with the two short edges. You may need to trim some of the fabric away from the corners to give a neater finish.

6 Apply the self-adhesive felt to the larger piece of card, smoothing down as you go to ensure there are no creases or bubbles. (Or use ordinary felt attached with double-sided tape.)

7 On the back of the card mark a point 2.5cm (1in) from the top and 5cm (2in) from one side. Repeat on the opposite side. Place a strip of double-sided tape from the mark to the top of the card, fold the gold ribbon in half and press each end onto the tape. For a neat finish cover the ends with small strips of adhesive felt.

8 Referring to the photograph for placement, add the stitched piece and stars. I used foam sticky pads for the large stars to give a raised effect.

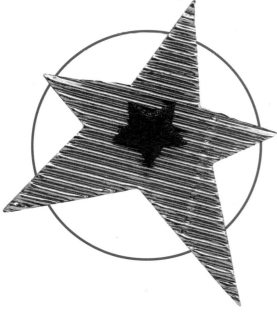

Ready-made stars, available from card-making suppliers, provide a finishing touch of glamour.

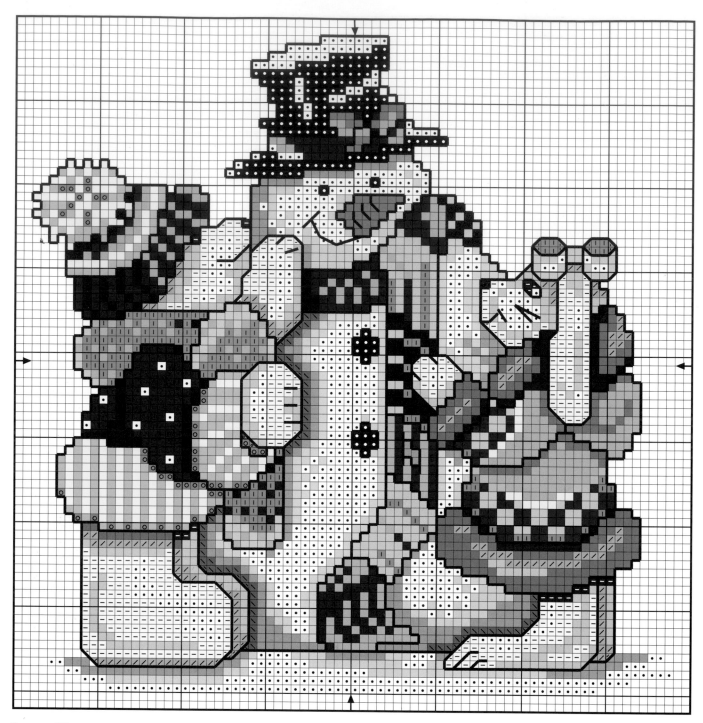

Snow Characters

DMC stranded cotton

Cross stitch

• blanc	340	435	738	− 838	993
208	341	⁄ 437	740	905	○ 3852
209	351	− 712	∟ 762	907	
310	415	725	815	⦀ 3746	
318	433	727	817	3814	

Backstitch
— 838

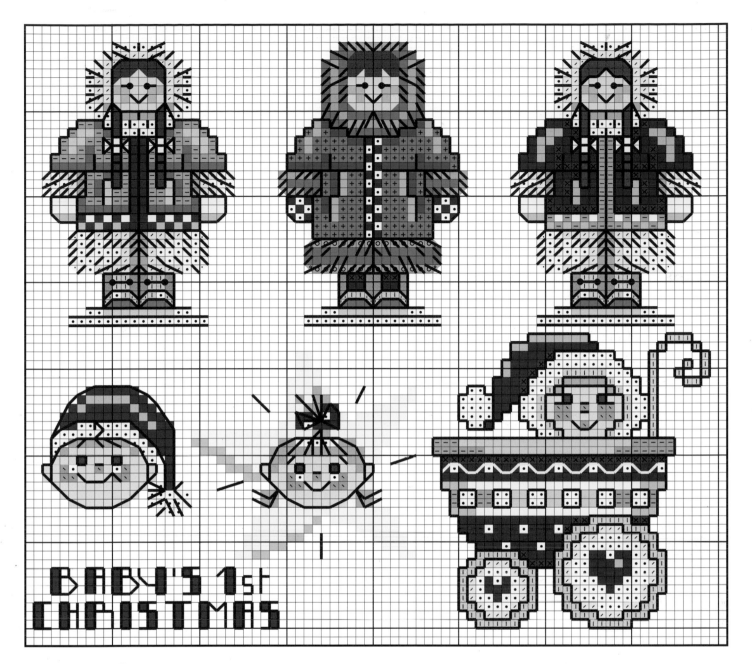

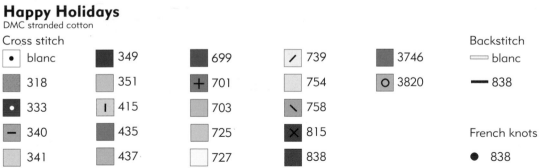

Happy Holidays
DMC stranded cotton

Cross stitch

• blanc		349		699	/	739		3746
	318		351	+	701		754	○	3820
⊡ 333	I	415		703	\	758		
— 340		435		725	✕	815		
	341		437		727		838		

Backstitch

⊂⊃ blanc

— 838

French knots

● 838

Snowy Cheer

DMC stranded cotton

Cross stitch

•	blanc		349	L	437		725	✗	815		3746
⊙	310		352		611		727		838		3747
	318		415	T	612	✓	738		3345		
	340		434		613		754	+	3347		
—	341	O	435	＼	712		783		3348		

Backstitch
— 838
— 3746

French knots
● 838

Santa and Friends

Christmas can sometimes seem a long way off for little ones, so help them count down the days with this lovely advent calendar. Holding onto his hat as his reindeer and sleigh zoom across a moonlit sky, Santa has plenty of goodies in his sacks. Below him the lights are still on in the houses and in between are the advent days stitched on tiny pockets for a small gift or sweet. To accompany this design there are several small projects – a card, gift tag, gift box and plaque design.

You will need

- Mid-blue 28-count evenweave fabric 26 x 31cm (10 x 12in) for the upper section and 18 x 31cm (7 x 12in) for the lower section (you may wish to cut the fabric smaller if you are making the pictures into the advent calendar)
- DMC stranded cotton (floss) as listed in the key, including three skeins of white
- Fine gold cord, ribbon, thread or similar for the reins
- Tapestry needle size 26
- Materials for making a wall hanging as listed on page 66

Design size: Upper: 16 x 21cm (6¼ x 8¼in)
Lower: 9 x 21cm (3½ x 8¼in)
Stitch count: Upper: 90 high x 116 wide
Lower: 50 high x 116 wide

Opposite: If you wish to use this design as a picture you can work the two large images together, omitting the lower and upper borders of the top and bottom pictures respectively. Notice that the wisp of smoke from the chimney of the house at the bottom right rises up into the sky below Santa's sleigh. Use this to align your two pictures.

1 Find and mark the centre of the fabric for each section of the design. Starting in the centre and following the chart on pages 64–65, begin by working the cross stitch in two strands over two threads of the fabric.

2 Work all the backstitch in one strand of the colours listed in the key.

3 Use gold cord or similar for the reins on the sleigh. Ideally work in a frame to keep the fabric taut as you position them. The placement is shown on the charts by black dots and you can also refer to the colour photograph opposite. Knot one end of the thread and bring your needle up on the harness of the reindeer in the foreground. Pull the thread taut and push the needle back in at the dot on Santa's glove. To loop the reins in his hand bring the thread to the front of the fabric at the dot on top of his glove. Push the needle to the back about one stitch away but hold the thread with your finger to form a loop. Arrange the loop and catch it with a few stitches to secure it before making the second rein.

4 Once the reins are in place, use a matching thread to take small stitches over each one at intervals to secure it. Ideally confine these stitches to the ends of the reins to hold them taut and give a nice effect.

5 When you have completed all the stitching follow the instructions on page 66 to make a wall hanging.

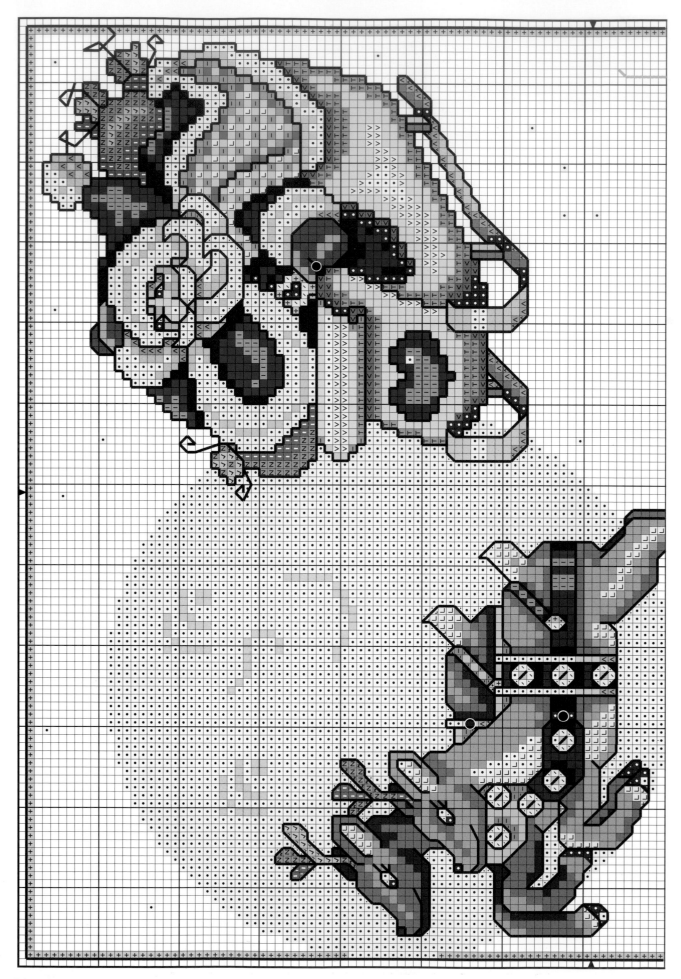

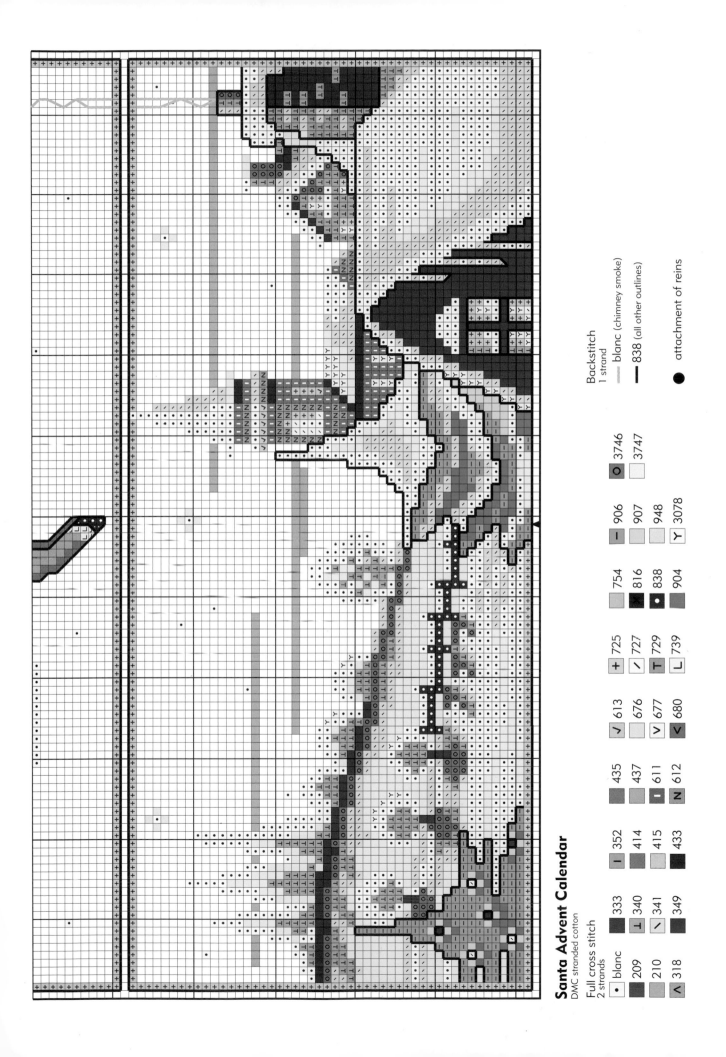

Santa Advent Calendar
DMC stranded cotton

Full cross stitch
2 strands

• blanc	I 352	I 435
209	⊥ 340	437
210	∕ 341	I 611
< 318	333	N 612

+ 725	I 906	O 3746
∕ 727	I 907	3747
T 729	948	
L 739	Y 3078	

∕ 613	754
676	816
V 677	⊙ 838
∨ 680	904

349	433
415	

Backstitch
1 strand

— blanc (chimney smoke)
— 838 (all other outlines)

● attachment of reins

Advent Calendar Wall Hanging

FOR THE POCKETS

- Six lengths of white gold-edged 14-count Aida bands 5 x 23cm (2 x 9in)
- DMC cotton (floss) as listed in key on page 65 including two skeins of white and dark brown (838)
- Tapestry needle size 26
- Six strips of iron-on interfacing to match the Aida bands

FOR THE WALL HANGING

- The two stitched pictures worked from the chart on pages 64–65
- Two pieces of felt for the wall hanging 38 x 76cm (15 x 30in)
- 1.25m (1½yd) iron-on interfacing
- Two 'D' rings
- Three skeins of contrasting stranded cotton for the blanket stitch edging (optional)
- Sewing machine or usual sewing equipment

Stitching the pockets

1 Mark the bands on the Aida with the positions of the pockets. Each motif is centred in a space of 31 stitches and there are four to each band. Count the spaces carefully and mark with a pin. You will need to leave about seven stitches at each end for hems. Check the spacing, then tack (baste) along the dividing lines.

2 To avoid confusion stitch all the numbers first in backstitch, referring to the chart on page 71. I used two strands of 838 for these to give definition.

3 Now work the motifs following the order in the photograph on page 63 or working in any order you prefer and referring to the charts on pages 70–71. Begin your stitching in the middle of each space. Work the cross stitch in two strands of thread.

4 Work all the backstitch outlines and French knots in one strand of 838 or 352.

5 When all the bands are complete, iron the interfacing to the back and press small hems under. This will strengthen your work and give a neat and professional finish. Do not remove your tacking (basting) at this stage. It is useful when attaching the pockets to the wall hanging.

Making the wall hanging

1 The easiest way to attach the main pictures is by giving them a frayed edge. On the wrong side of the fabric carefully measure 12mm (½in) around the stitched border and mark with a soft pencil. Add a line of stay stitching just outside the yellow cross stitched border. Trim the fabric to the pencil line and then fray the edges. The fabric will only fray up to the line of stitching, leaving an attractive border.

I used fine twisted cord for Santa's reins, catching it in place with a few discreet matching stitches.

2 Cut two pieces of iron-on interfacing to fit the back of each stitched picture, making sure they will not overlap the frayed edges. Fuse to the back of each cross stitched piece.

3 Cut one piece of interfacing the same size as one of your felt rectangles and fuse to the back.

4 Lay the interfaced felt out on a flat surface. Lay the upper part of the design on top. I placed mine centrally with the stitched border 3cm (1¼in) from the top edge of the felt. This leaves a border of felt about 9cm (3½in) on each side. Pin in place.

5 Measure 20cm (8in) from the top of the felt and position the first row of pockets centrally. The long edge of the band can be lined up with the lower border of the picture. Now lay out the remaining strips, leaving about 12mm (½in) between each band. Take your time getting this right and adjust as necessary. Finally, place the lower picture below the pockets. Pin everything in position.

6 Stitch the main picture in place with matching thread. Now attach the bands. It is easier to stitch the vertical lines on the pockets first and then the horizontal line at the bottom. Use contrasting cotton for definition and follow your original tacking lines. Finally, stitch the lower picture in place.

7 Lay the two felt pieces together, right sides out, and topstitch all round about 1cm (⅜in) away from the edge. If desired, work a decorative border of blanket stitch around the edge, using the line of top-stitching as a guide. This is optional because the felt will never fray.

8 Attach two 'D' rings to the back, fill the pockets with chocolate coins or other small goodies and your advent calendar is ready to use. After use, roll up the calendar and store it in a pillowcase. The felt ensures a robust construction that will allow many years of enjoyment for generations of children.

This section from the bottom of the advent calendar makes an attractive design in its own right and could be worked alone and framed or applied to the front of any fabric item to give it some Christmas flair.

Gifts For All

As Christmas draws nearer it is time to think about sending cards and wrapping presents for the special people in your life. A decorative Santa plaque (opposite) makes a lovely present and a cross stitch tag or gift box show how much you care. Make something for yourself too, like the Christmas card list notebook, below.

Blank card or papier-mâchè items are a great basis for embroidery. This pretty box is made of papier mâché, and I painted it white and added the red fabric hearts and ribbon trims for decoration. The box is 7cm (2¾in) in diameter with a 4cm (1¾in) aperture and it is 4cm (1¾in) deep, so it could hold a piece of jewellery, a small ornament or even the key to something much bigger. I used silver 14-count perforated paper for the stitching, which has a lovely metallic sheen, and I omitted the backstitch from the design (see page 70) for a delicate look. Use the lid liner as a template to trim the design to fit and glue in place with mini glue dots or clear glue.

A hand-stitched gift tag is always appreciated, especially if, like this one, Santa's helpers may have made it. I worked the design from page 73 on 28-count cream evenweave fabric and then stiffened it with PVA glue (see page 98) so I could cut it out without it fraying. I made the card myself, shaping the top edge for added detail, though you can buy a blank to work on. For the tying string I used an ordinary hole-punch and then decorated the hole with a laser-cut sticker, but you could use a standard reinforcement ring and paint it silver. To stick the design to the card use mini glue dots, double-sided tape or clear glue.

This delightful project is simple to make using a ready-made notebook with an aperture for your embroidery. All you have to do is stitch the design, trim the fabric to fit and stick it behind the aperture with double-sided tape. I used cream 14-count Aida with gold Lurex thread for a festive look. Decorate the cover with gold stars and use a metallic marker to write 'Christmas Card List' on the front. The post-box design for this notebook is on page 71.

Santa Plaque

You will need

- Cream 14-count perforated paper 12 x 15cm (4¾ x 6in)
- DMC stranded cotton (floss) as listed in the key
- Tapestry needle size 26
- Varnished, sliced-wood wall plaque about 20 x 10cm (8 x 4in) at its widest points (available from craft shops and floristry suppliers)
- Small wired 'twig' star (optional)
- Adhesive foam pads
- Sharp scissors
- Pencil and ruler
- Mini glue dots or clear glue
- Picture ring for hanging

1 Use a ruler to find the centre of the perforated paper. Following the chart on page 73, begin by working the cross stitch in two strands.

2 Work all the backstitch using one strand of 838.

3 Using sharp scissors and following the line of the stitching as closely as possible, cut out your Santa figure. Do not attempt to cut away the paper behind his walking stick or between his boots.

4 Attach several of the sticky foam pads to the back of the stitching and then position your Santa on the plaque and press firmly into place. The pads raise the stitched piece slightly above the surface.

5 Add the twig star using mini glue dots or a spot of glue. Attach a picture ring to the back so you can hang the plaque.

Perforated paper is ideal for this project because it won't fray when you cut out the stitched design and it is protected by the wooden backing.

'Tis the season…

… to keep up with the times

My Santa is worked in the traditional colours but you can work his robes in, say, blues or purples to match your room scheme, if preferred, and introduce a modern twist by replacing the twig star with one made of metal or beaded wire.

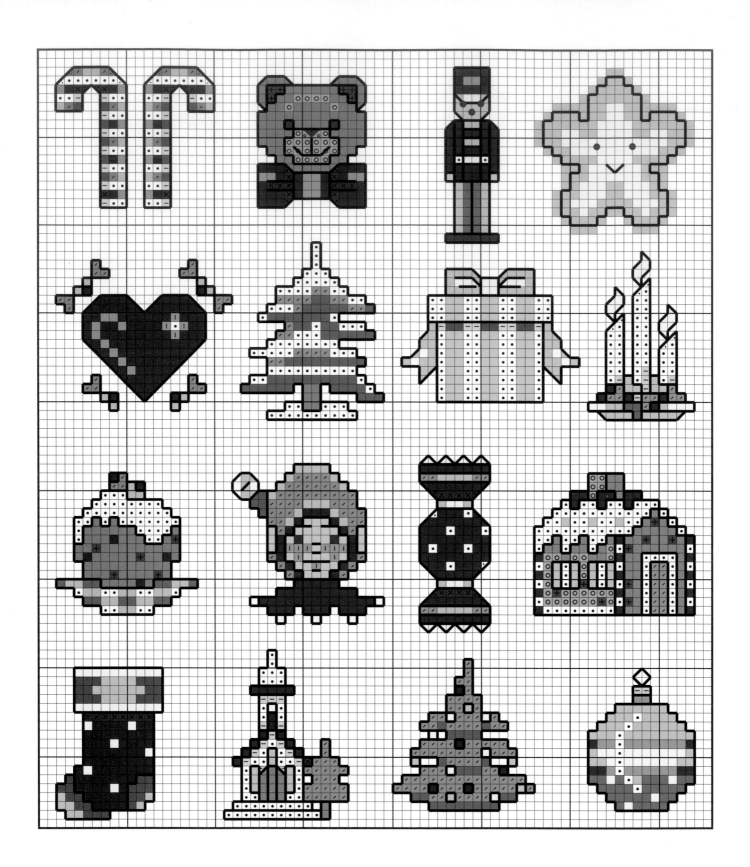

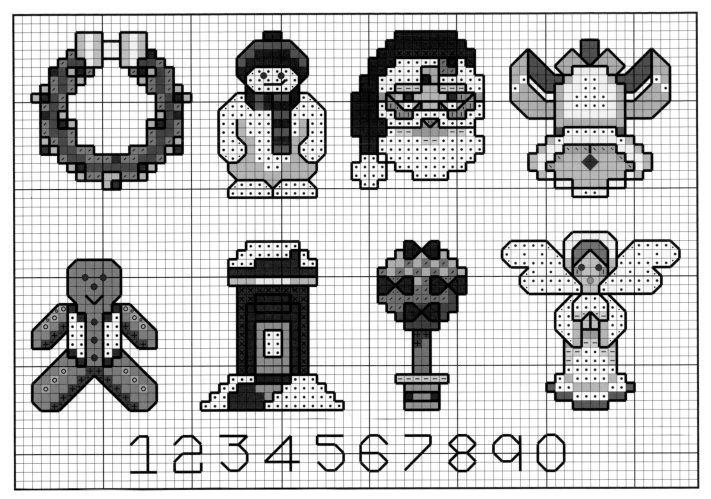

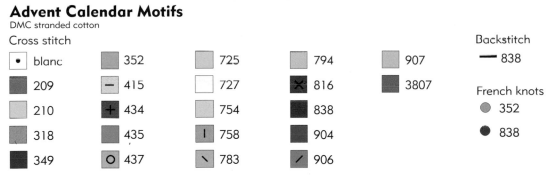

Advent Calendar Motifs

DMC stranded cotton

Cross stitch

•	blanc		352		725		794		907
	209	−	415		727	✖	816		3807
	210	+	434		754		838		
	318		435	ǀ	758		904		
	349	⊙	437	＼	783	／	906		

Backstitch

— 838

French knots

● 352

● 838

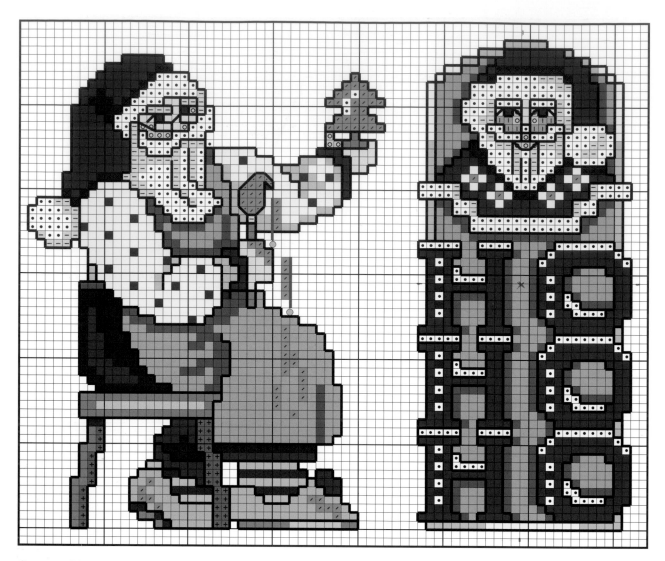

Santa Claus

DMC stranded cotton

Cross stitch

• blanc	◪ 435	L 739	▫ 948	
◪ 340	＼ 553	O 754	◼ 3345	
◼ 350	▫ 725	I 758	／ 3347	
— 415	▫ 727	◼ 816	◪ 3348	
+ 434	▫ 738	◼ 838	◼ 3746	

Backstitch

— 838

— 3345

French knots

● 3348

Toys, Toys, Toys
DMC stranded cotton

Cross stitch

•	blanc		437	I	772	■	838
■	351		725		783		948
–	415		727		798	■	3345
+	434	L	739	✕	815	╱	3347
	435	O	754	■	817		3348

Backstitch

— 838

French knots

● 838

Feast of Christmas

Turkey with all the trimmings, Christmas cake, fruit pudding, mulled wine and family specialities can become such a tradition that the mere mention of them brings back memories of previous festivities. The aroma of nutmeg or cinnamon still reminds me of watching my mother make Christmas cake when I'd stand on a chair helping her weigh and stir ingredients into our huge old mixing bowl. Gingerbread is another distinctive taste associated with the holiday, so I've illustrated this section with a gingerbread house complete with candy canes, and there is a selection of table accessories to run alongside it.

You will need

- Pale lemon 14-count Aida 36 x 36cm (14 x 14in)
- DMC stranded cotton (floss) including two skeins of white as listed in the key
- Tapestry needle size 26
- Mount board and picture frame

Design size: 21 x 20cm (8¼ x 8in)
Stitch count: 114 high x 110 wide

1 Find and mark the centre of the Aida. Starting in the centre and following the chart on pages 78–79, begin by working the cross stitch in two strands.

2 Work all the backstitch and French knots in one strand of 838.

3 When you have completed all the stitching, wash and press your work and prepare it for framing following the instructions on page 102.

'Tis the season...

... to start with something simple
This design is particularly suitable for a beginner because there are very few partial stitches. If desired use beads or gold thread to highlight particular areas.

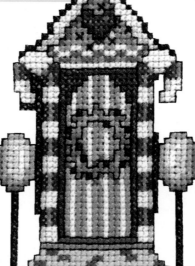

Opposite: I've used a lovely bright shade of lemon as the background for this design. The colours of the gingerbread show up particularly well against it, giving a lively look and making this design suitable as a year-round picture for a child's room.

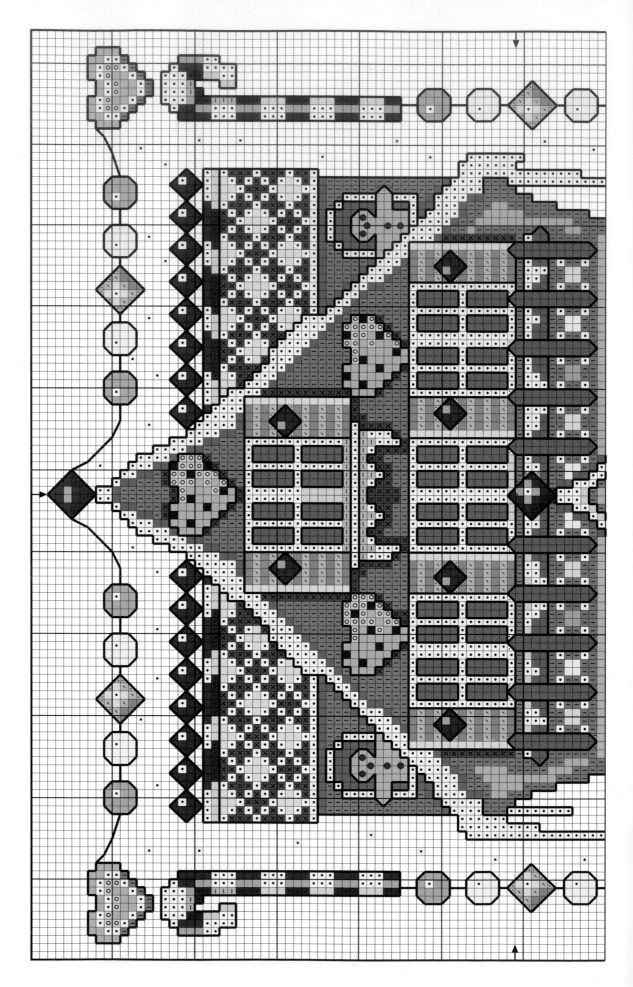

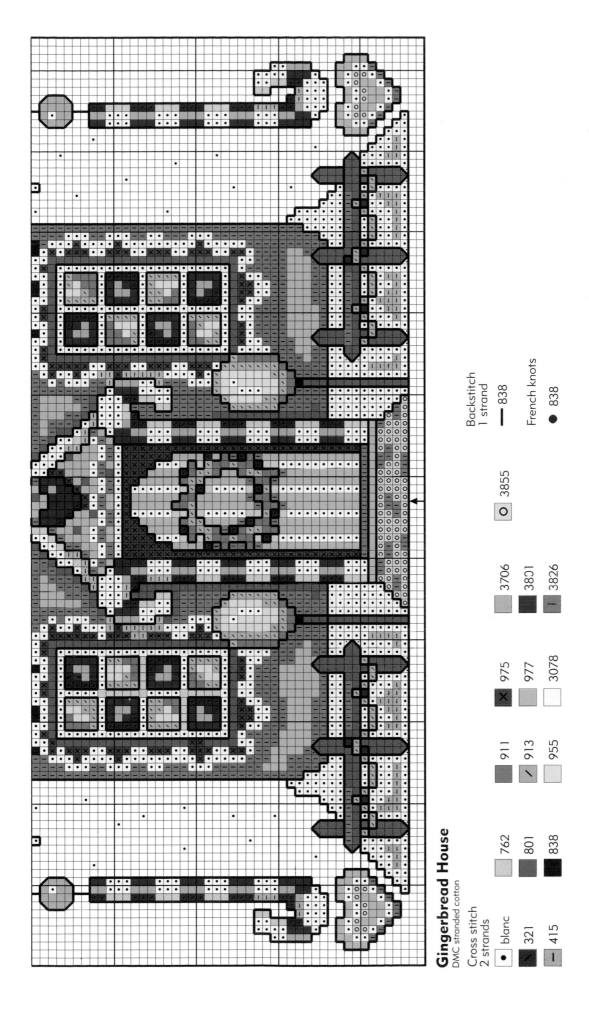

Gingerbread House
DMC stranded cotton

Cross stitch
2 strands

•	blanc			
╱	321			
		415		
	762			
	801			
✕	838			

✕	911	
╱	913	
	955	
	975	
	977	
	3078	

	3706
	3801
	3826

○	3855

Backstitch
1 strand
—— 838

French knots
● 838

Seasonal Table

Give Santa a snack to keep him going, with a plate of mince pies and perhaps a little something to drink. A tray cloth with a thank-you message would welcome the honoured visitor, and it can become one of your family traditions to use it every year. The preservative bands could be another tradition, along with the coaster and napkin ring, which are quick enough to make for all your guests.

Napkin rings like these are usually supplied in kits, complete with 14-count vinyl weave fabric cut to size. All you have to do is work your design in the centre and then insert the fabric back into the ring. I used one of the square 'tile' designs from a border on page 86 and a design on page 87 for the serviette holder, worked on another square of vinyl weave. For the coaster I combined the napkin ring design with a heart and holly-leaf edging from another pattern on the same page. When combining patterns like this it helps if you transfer the designs onto graph paper, cut them out and arrange them until you have a pleasing effect.

Santa's Tray Cloth

You will need

- 28-count evenweave fabric 20 x 18cm (8 x 7in)
- DMC stranded cotton (floss) as listed in the key
- Tapestry needle size 26
- Co-ordinating fabric 30 x 46cm (12 x 18in)
- Plain fabric for backing 30 x 46cm (12 x 18in) – see step 6
- Ruler
- Pencil
- Sewing machine or usual sewing equipment

1 Find and mark the centre of the evenweave fabric. Starting in the centre and following the chart on page 89, work the cross stitch in two strands over two threads of fabric.

2 Work all the backstitch in the design using one strand of 838.

3 On the wrong side of the design, use a ruler to measure a 2.5cm (1in) border around the stitching and mark lightly with a line of pencil dots. This will be your stitching line when attaching the design to the backing fabric. Measure another line 12mm (½in) beyond this to form your cutting line.

4 Cut out the stitched piece following your cutting line. Press firmly, turning the hem allowance back to the dotted stitching line on the wrong side.

5 Position the stitched piece in the bottom left-hand corner of the co-ordinating fabric. Do not to place it too close to the edge as you need to allow for the two pieces of the tray cloth fabric to be joined together. Pin in place and stitch around all the edges.

6 With right sides together and taking a 6mm (¼in) seam allowance, stitch the co-ordinating and plain backing fabrics together, leaving an opening at the side for turning. I used curtain lining for my backing, which gives an excellent finish.

7 Turn the tray cloth right sides out and press it. You can either slipstitch the opening closed or finish as I did with a line of contrasting topstitching.

This mince pie looks good enough to eat and might even be an inspiration for fine cooking.

'Tis the season...

... to make use of Aida bands

Stitch decorative designs from this book onto Aida bands and use them to edge a tray cloth made from festive fabric. These are quick to stitch and you can have a lot of fun combining several of the smaller designs in this book.

Preserve Bands

You will need

FOR THE HEART BAND

- White, red-edged 14-count Aida band 5cm (2in) wide – 35cm (13¾in) will easily fit an 822g jar but for other sizes measure the jar to see how long it should be, adding extra for a small hem and overlap
- Iron-on interfacing the same size as the Aida band (optional)

FOR THE CHECKED BAND

- White 14-count vinyl weave 7.5cm (3in) square
- Two pieces of red checked fabric 9 x 35cm (3½ x 13¾in)
- Iron-on interfacing 9 x 35cm (3½ x 13¾in)
- Pencil
- Ruler
- Clear glue

FOR EACH BAND

- DMC stranded cotton (floss) as listed in the key
- Tapestry needle size 26
- Two Velcro spots
- Scissors
- Usual sewing equipment

1 Find and mark the centre of the Aida band. Starting in the centre and following the appropriate chart on page 86, work the cross stitch in two strands. Repeat the border of holly leaves above the heart design.

2 For the checked band work all the backstitch in one strand of 838 except the lettering for which I used two strands for definition. Use sharp scissors to trim the checked band design, leaving a border of two squares of vinyl weave.

3 To finish the heart band press the embroidery and press under a small hem at each end. Iron interfacing to the back (optional). Stitch the hems and add two Velcro spots to fasten the band, ensuring that these are positioned so the band will be held taut around the jar.

4 For the checked band iron interfacing onto the wrong side of one of the checked fabric pieces. Place right sides together with the other strip and stitch together all round, taking a 6mm (¼in) seam allowance and leaving an opening at the bottom.

5 Clip the seam allowances at the corners, turn the band out and press it. Slipstitch the opening closed. Attach Velcro spots, ensuring that they are positioned to hold the band taut around the jar. Use a ruler to find the centre of the fabric and mark with a pin. Use this to position your stitched piece, sticking it in place with a little clear glue.

'Tis the season...

... to make your own labels

Homemade jams are traditionally labelled with the contents and date. A nice idea would be to stitch this information on your label. Cover the lid with a circle of gingham and secure with ribbon to complete the farmhouse look.

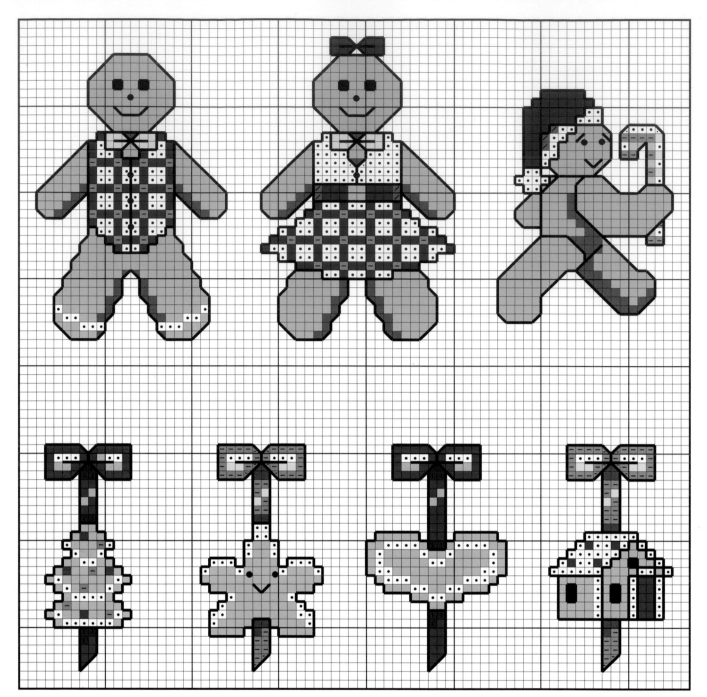

Gingerbread Treats

DMC stranded cotton

Cross stitch

•	blanc		838		3706
	168		909	O	3826
	498	—	912		3827
	666		955		
/	801		975		

Backstitch

— 838

French knots

● 838

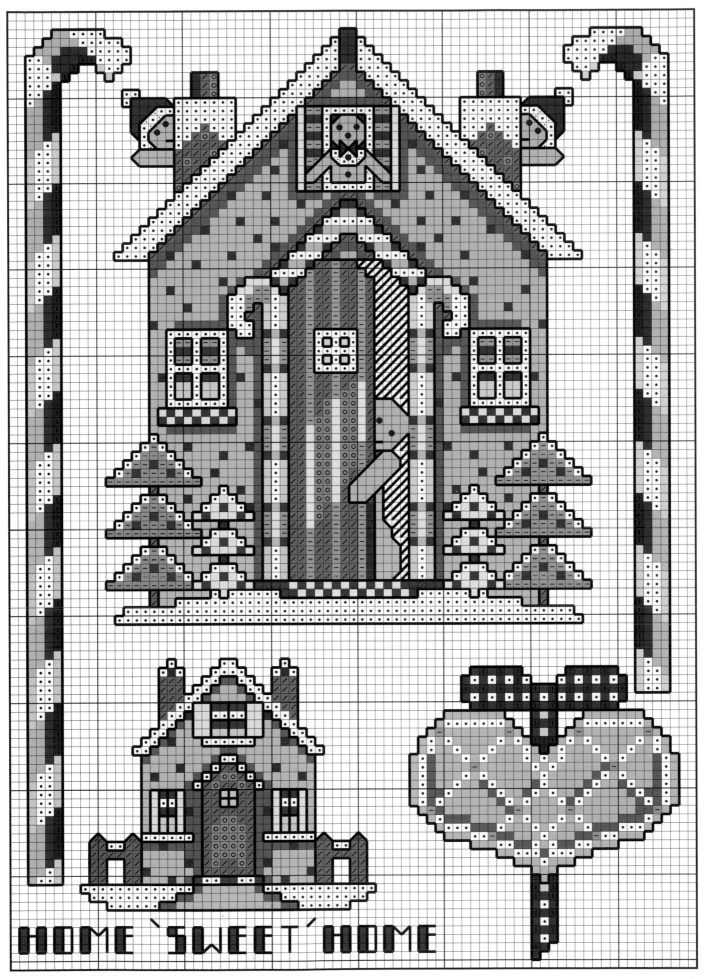

Festive Kitchen
DMC stranded cotton

Cross stitch

•	blanc		415	╱	677	—	739	
O	318		434		700		741	
	349	I	435		703		838	
X	351	╲	437		725			
	352		676		727			

Backstitch
— 349
— 838

French knots
● 838

A Taste of Christmas

DMC stranded cotton

Cross stitch

• blanc	433	727	910		
340	I 435	738	913		
349	437	/ 746	3746		
351	498	783			
415	725	838			

Backstitch

— 783
— 838

Alphabets and Greetings

Initials or personalized messages make embroidery extra special, but embroiderers are often put off by the idea of having to position the letters themselves. Don't be afraid; it is really easy if you follow the simple steps below. Try it for yourself using the festive alphabets on the following pages or use them straight off the page, sampler style, to improve your confidence.

You will need

- Graph paper – I find that 10 squares to 2.5cm (1in) is by far the best for design purposes
- Pencil and eraser
- Ballpoint or felt-tip pen
- Ring binder or folder (optional)

'Tis the season...

... to consider changing the fabric count
If your wording doesn't fit comfortably in the space available, consider changing to a higher count fabric for your project. This is an especially useful idea for very small items such as pot lids, key rings or jewellery.

1 Take time to consider where to place the lettering on the fabric. Count the number of squares available for the lettering. Consider whether you want words to run horizontally or vertically.

2 Write out the words and choose a suitable scale alphabet to begin charting. Don't try arranging the words at this stage, simply chart them carefully, remembering to leave spaces between each word and using pencil so that you can make any necessary corrections. As a rule use an odd number of spaces between letters that occupy an odd number of squares and leave even-numbered spaces between even-numbered letters. This can be adjusted later, if needed, to improve the final look.

3 Count the total number of squares (including the spaces and any punctuation) that your words occupy. Divide the number in half to find the centre point and mark it with a dot.

4 Now use graph paper to mark out the area where your lettering will go. Find and mark the centre. Match it up with the centre of your words to see whether you need to make any adjustments. (When lettering is enclosed by a stitched border it usually looks best with an equal number of squares at each end.)

5 Once you are happy with the positioning of the words, you can use ink to go over the stitching lines. Store charted messages in a folder or ring binder to use again.

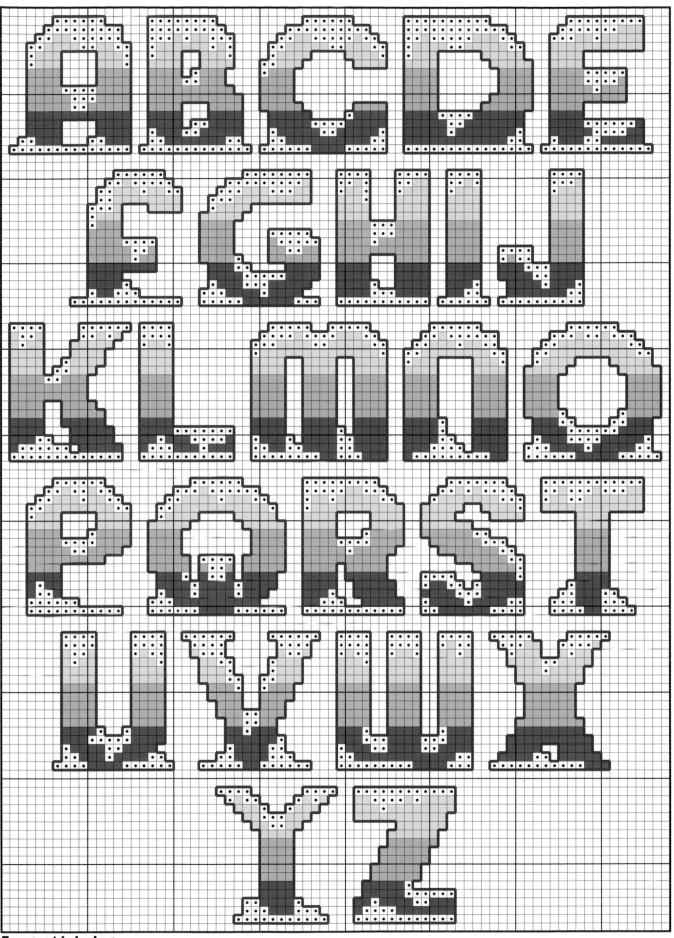

Frosty Alphabet
DMC stranded cotton
Cross stitch

		Backstitch
• blanc	▒ 340	▓ 3746	░ 3747	— 3746

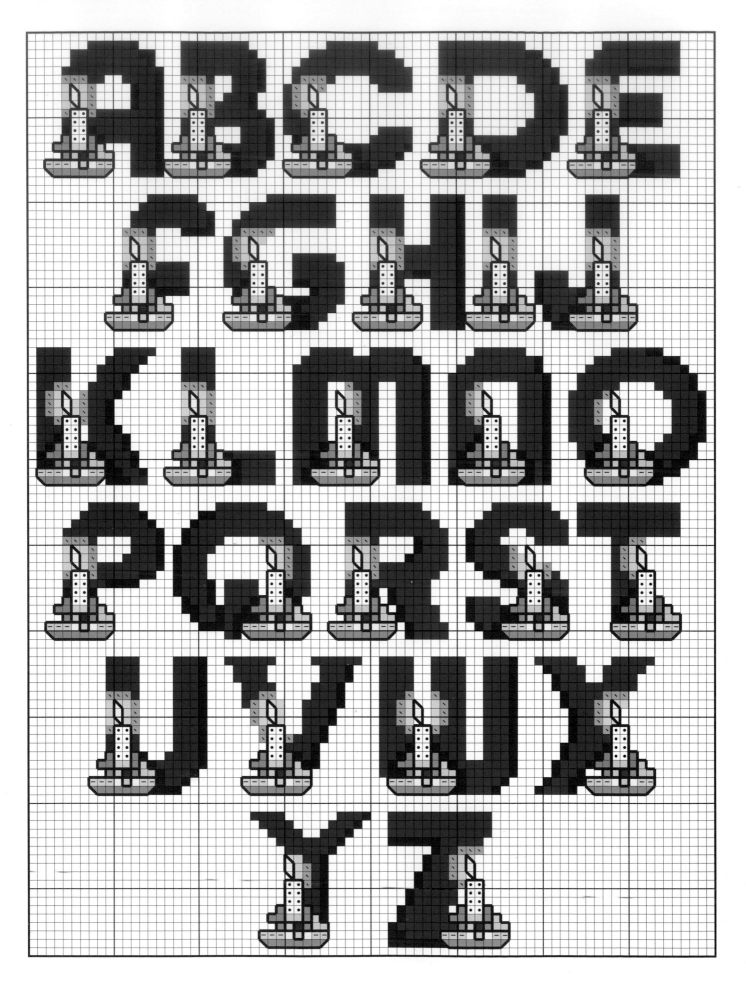

Warm and Welcoming Alphabets

DMC stranded cotton

Cross stitch

						Backstitch
• blanc	╲ 352	415	727	815	3348	— 838
349	353	— 725	783	3347		

Words of Good Cheer

DMC stranded cotton

Cross stitch

•	blanc	＼	352		437	−	739		743
	349		353		498		742		744

Backstitch
— 703
— 838

French knots
● 349

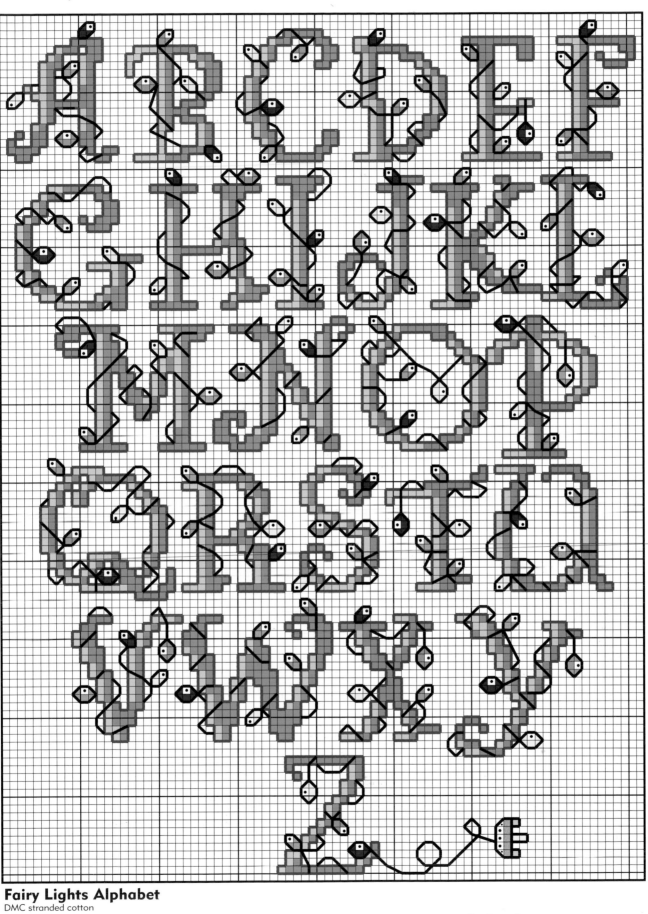

Fairy Lights Alphabet
DMC stranded cotton

Cross stitch

					Backstitch
• blanc	415	700	725	741	— 699
340	554	703	727	817	— 838

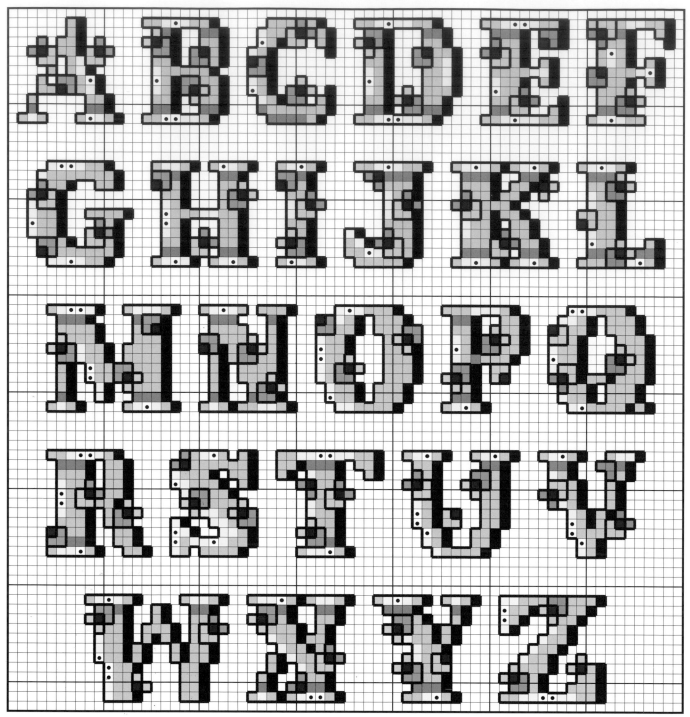

Golden Holly Alphabet
DMC stranded cotton

Cross stitch

- • blanc
- 703
- 727
- 817
- 700
- 725
- 815
- 3820

Backstitch
- — 838

Materials and Equipment

There are a few things you need to buy when starting out in cross stitch, and some items that need to be bought for each project, but as you progress you'll find that you very soon build up a collection of basics and a stock of threads.

Fabric

Most of the large designs in this book have been worked on Aida or evenweave fabric, which has the same number of horizontal and vertical threads per inch, making it very easy to count and ensuring that every stitch is the same size.

Aida is made from 100 per cent cotton and is woven in regular, clearly defined blocks to make stitching easy. One stitch is made over one block, using the holes in the fabric as a guide. Aida comes in several counts, 11, 14, 16 and 18 being the standard sizes. The count refers to the number of blocks (or stitches) per inch on the fabric. The higher the number of blocks, the smaller the design will be. Most of the designs in this book have been stitched on 14-count Aida. To make the design smaller, work on a higher count fabric.

Evenweave fabric has the same number of warp and weft threads and a regular pattern of holes. It looks much finer than Aida but each cross stitch is worked over two threads and as a result a project sewn on 28-count evenweave fabric will come out the same size as one stitched on 14-count Aida.

Perforated paper, as its name suggests, is a paper with holes punched in it for stitching. The benefit of using this paper is that it doesn't fray when cut so it is ideal for small projects, such as the Tree Treasures (page 26). Make sure you only choose motifs with whole stitches because this paper is not suitable for fractional stitches.

Vinyl weave can be used in the same way as perforated paper and is also only suitable for whole stitches. Its advantage is that it is stiff and washable. Use it for coasters (see page 80), jar labels or a serviette holder.

Needles and Threads

Use a blunt needle that slips easily through the fabric without piercing it. A size 24 or 26 tapestry needle is best for stitching the designs in this book.

All the projects in this book are stitched with DMC stranded cottons (floss) but a conversion table for Anchor threads is given on page 104. Cross stitch usually requires two strands, while backstitch and French knots are worked with one unless otherwise stated.

Some of the designs feature a combination of two types of thread. In the Nativity picture (page 35) for example, gold metallic thread combines with yellow to add a rich glow to the border. Thread one strand of each type of thread in the needle and stitch as normal. When using these special threads it is best to keep lengths fairly short to avoid tangling.

Rayon thread is very shiny and slippery, and dampening it slightly before threading your needle makes it easier to work with. Metallic thread should be knotted onto the eye of your needle together with the stranded cotton to help prevent it slipping and tangling.

Hoops and frames

Large projects benefit from being held taut while stitching is in progress. Always remove your projects from the hoop at the end of the day to prevent a ring mark forming.

Scissors

You will need at least two pairs of scissors: one large pair to cut the fabric to size and a small pair of sharp-pointed embroidery scissors to cut the threads. When making cards and other similar items you should also have paper scissors.

This neat serviette holder is decorated with the design on page 87 worked on a 7.5cm (3in) square of vinyl weave. I painted the wooden serviette holder red for a festive look.

Basic Techniques

Here is all the basic information you need to complete the projects in this book plus some advice on modifications you can make to personalize your work. Even if you are proficient at cross stitch you should read this section for advice specific to the projects.

Reading the charts

Colour charts are provided for all the projects in this book with each square representing one cross stitch. The key shows the colour of the stitch and lists the number of the DMC stranded cotton (floss) to use. Additional symbols have been given to some colours for further clarity. Half cross stitches are listed separately in the key for your convenience. Follow the key closely and work all the areas of full cross stitch first to avoid confusion. The smaller charts on each spread share a key, so check which colours you need before buying.

Backstitch is shown in a stronger colour in the key and chart than the actual shade used for clarity. French knots appear as small coloured dots and beads are shown as larger spheres. These too are sometimes shown in heightened colours. All these elements are listed separately in the key to help you follow the chart with ease.

Using the small motifs

The small designs in each chapter are quick to stitch and provide an excellent resource of ideas for cards, gifts and keepsakes. These can be stitched on fabric in the usual way or you can work on perforated paper or vinyl weave so that motifs can be cut out. Another idea is to stiffen the fabric with PVA glue, which allows you to choose designs with

fractional stitches. I used this method to make the Angel Tree Topper (page 27 and right).

Stiffening fabric with PVA glue Work your embroidery in the usual way and then use a stiff brush to cover the back of the fabric with an even coat of PVA glue. Cut a piece of backing fabric the same size and place it on the back of the embroidery, smoothing out any air bubbles. Add another coat of PVA glue to the surface of the backing and leave it to dry, overnight if possible. When dry, the fabric will be stiff but still pliable. Now coat the front of your stitching with an even covering of PVA glue. The glue will dry clear and once the front is dry the piece will be firm enough to cut out.

Adding your own input

Sometimes the smaller designs in this book may inspire your own ideas. You might think one would suit your purposes better on a different type or colour of fabric, when worked at a different size or when combined with one of the other designs in the book. Here are some pointers to help you make such adjustments.

Making a design larger or smaller is most easily done by changing the fabric count (see page 7). To calculate how large the motif will be on a given fabric you need to know the stitch count. This is given for the large pictures and some of the bigger motifs, but for the smaller projects you will need to count the number of stitches on the chart. If you are working over two strands of evenweave fabric, remember to halve the stitch count of the fabric – 28-count evenweave fabric is equivalent to 14-count Aida. Allow enough extra fabric for your finishing technique.

Changing the fabric colour can have a major impact, but it must be done carefully. The fabric colour forms an integral part of the Winter Wonderland (page 49) and Santa and Friends (page 63) pictures. Although all of the other main designs could quite easily be stitched on cream Aida, the feel of these two projects would be lost without the distinctive shades of fabric I've chosen to enhance the subjects.

Rich red and green fabrics look very tempting but often these colours clash badly with the stitching or you may find

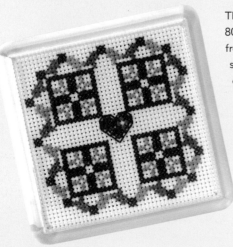

This coaster (see page 80) combines motifs from three designs very successfully and is an example of what can be achieved. When combining designs in this way it is always best to re-chart them on graph paper before you begin the stitching.

I used PVA glue to stiffen the fabric of this Angel Tree Topper so that it could be cut out and would stand up straight on the tree (see page 27).

areas of stitching simply 'disappearing' into the background. A subtle contrast gives a festive look without overwhelming your design.

I also resist using white because it can make even the most beautiful shades of thread look harsh. When in doubt always choose antique creams for projects using traditional reds, greens and golds. Slightly darker fabrics will give an heirloom look to any project. Rustico and the new 'antiqued' Aidas are perfect for achieving this slightly aged, country look.

Changing the motif is a matter of checking the stitch count as above to calculate the finished size. If you wish, you can combine designs as I did on the coaster (page 80) but to do this it is helpful to chart your new design in the same way as when adding lettering (see page 90).

Making your own tassels

Co-ordinated tassels are a perfect embellishment for Christmas projects such as the tree ornament on page 26. Although you can buy them ready-made, it will cost you nothing to make your own and I find the method explained here both easy and fun.

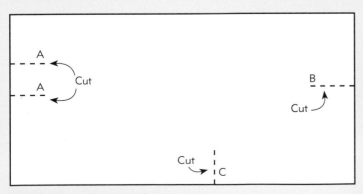

Template for making a tassel

1 Trace the template (below left) onto medium-weight card. Using a ruler and fine felt-tip pen, ink in all the markings and then cut out. You will need approximately 2m (2yd) of stranded cotton (floss) to make a tassel similar to the ones shown below.

2 Begin by taking a 23cm (9in) length of thread and knotting each end to prevent fraying. Double up the thread and secure the looped end in the A slots. Slide the knotted ends into the B slot.

3 Cut 1m (1yd) of thread and knot each end. Secure one end of this thread in slot C and begin to wrap it around the card. You are now making the body of the tassel and its finished size will depend on how many times you wrap the thread around the card. Once the tassel is the right size, secure the remaining end by sliding it into slot C.

4 Release the thread from slots A and B, slipping the knotted ends through the loop; pull tight. Slide the two knotted ends of thread from slot C and remove the card.

5 Cut another 23cm (9in) length of thread and tightly wind it around the tassel top. Finish with a double knot and cut the end of this thread close to the knot. Now hold the tassel firmly and use sharp scissors to trim it to the desired length.

This tree ornament (page 26) features three tassels made using the method described here.

Working the Stitches

Here are instructions on preparing your fabric and working the stitches
you need for the projects in this book. Follow the information carefully,
especially if you have not worked partial stitches before.

Preparing to stitch

As a general rule, cut your fabric at least 7.5cm (3in) larger all
round than the design size. Zigzag around the edges or bind
them with masking tape (not ordinary sticky tape) to prevent
fraying. Iron out any deep creases. Find the centre by folding
the fabric in four and marking with a pin or small stitch. On
the large designs follow the arrows from the edges of the
chart to the centre point, which you should match up with
your centre mark on the fabric. For the smaller motifs find the
centre of your chosen design by counting how many stitches
high and wide it is and dividing in half to find the middle. In
all cases make your first stitch at the centre of your fabric to
ensure the correct placement of your design.

Starting and finishing

Bring the needle up through the underside of the fabric and
leave about 2.5cm (1in) of thread, securing the tail with your
first few stitches. Finish off by running the thread under a
few stitches at the back and snip off the excess close to the
stitching with sharp-pointed embroidery scissors.

Cross stitch

Each cross stitch is worked over one block of Aida or two
threads of finer evenweave fabric. Starting at the centre of
your fabric and the centre of the chart, bring your needle up
at the bottom left corner of the block/square you want to fill
and push it down in the top right corner. Bring it up again
in the bottom right corner and push it down in the top left.
When working a block of stitches in the same colour, stitch
a line of half crosses and complete each cross on the return
journey. Make sure that the top half of each cross stitch lies
in the same direction.

Half cross stitch

Half cross stitch is useful for creating depth. Where half cross
stitch is used, the colours are listed separately in the keys on
the chart pages. A half cross stitch is the first part of a full
cross stitch worked over one block of Aida or two threads of
evenweave fabric from the bottom left to the top right corner.

Three-quarter stitches

Three-quarter stitches, also called fractional or partial
stitches, are used to create a smooth curve on the outlines
of some designs. On the charts these are shown as triangles
filling half a square (see diagram below) and any symbols
are smaller than usual. A three-quarter stitch is a half stitch
(the first part of a cross stitch) with a quarter stitch from one
corner to the centre of the stitch. Designs using lots of these
stitches are easiest to work over two threads of evenweave
fabric. (28-count evenweave fabric is equivalent to 14-count
Aida.) When using Aida you may need a separate sharp
needle to pierce the middle of the block to make your
three-quarter stitch.

Three-quarter stitch

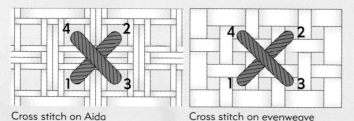

Cross stitch on Aida   Cross stitch on evenweave

Backstitch

This is an outlining stitch that can be worked diagonally, vertically or horizontally, usually once all the cross stitch has been completed. Bring the needle up from the underside and take it down one square back before coming up again one square in front of the line you have completed so far. Backstitch can be worked as single stitches over one or two threads of the fabric or as longer stitches to cover a larger area. Some of the smaller designs have been given the look of freehand drawings by using backstitch this way. The line does not always follow the grid or the cross stitches exactly from corner to corner. You will need to follow the chart carefully to re-create this effect. Bear in mind, however, that you are aiming for a 'sketchy' look so don't worry if your backstitching is not exactly the same, as long as you try to retain the shape and feel of the motif.

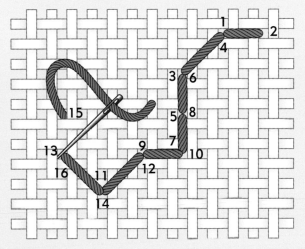

Backstitch

French knots

French knots are used to add details such as eyes and noses and are shown on the charts as small dots. There are several methods of working them but I find this one the easiest. Bring

Starting a French knot

the needle up through the fabric, then holding the thread taut in your left hand, wrap the needle around it twice. Now push the needle back into the fabric close to where it came up, making sure you keep the thread taut. Gently pull the needle and thread until a neat knot is formed on the front. If you have never worked this stitch before spend some time practising on a scrap of fabric first.

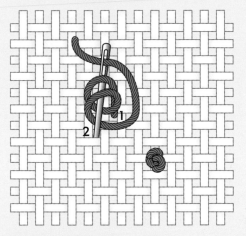

Completing a French knot

Beads

I've used beads to enhance the Victorian Christmas Tree design (page 21) and they are clearly shown on the chart. Many of the motifs lend themselves to being stitched either completely or partly in beads. To do this, simply substitute areas of stitching for beads of a similar colour. Beads are added with a half cross stitch. Bring the needle up in the bottom left corner, thread a bead on your needle and take it down in the top right. To secure the bead firmly, work the top half of the cross stitch (back through the centre of the bead) as well.

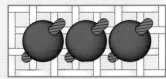

Attaching beads

All the basic stitches are combined in this gorgeous design from the Traditional Christmas chapter (chart on page 14). The motif is worked in cross stitch with backstitch for detailing. The letters combine cross stitch and backstitch with French knots. I worked the design on 18-count Aida.

Finishing Touches

Once you have completed the stitching you'll want to present your embroidery properly
and keep it in the best possible condition. The following information will set you on track.

Cleaning and pressing

Keep your work as clean as possible at all times. This means
keeping your hands clean when working and storing the
piece carefully between stitching sessions – a pillowcase is
good for storing large designs in progress. However, even
the natural oils in your skin can dull the lustre of the threads
so it's always worth washing your finished work. Use a mild
detergent in warm water and rinse the embroidery thoroughly.
In the unlikely event that colours begin to bleed, keep rinsing
until the water runs completely clear, and then roll the
embroidery in a towel to remove excess water; never wring it.
Press, using a medium setting on your iron, with the work face
down on a thick towel to prevent the stitches flattening. Iron
until dry. Take extra care when ironing projects with beads or
metallic thread.

Mounting and framing

I would always recommend that you take large designs to
a professional framer. Not only will they be able to give you
excellent advice regarding the best choice of mounts and
frames to enhance your work, but they will also be able to
ensure the piece is stretched perfectly first.

Many of the main projects in this book may only be brought
out once a year as accents to your Christmas decoration. So
to ensure that they are destined to become family favourites
for years to come it's vitally important they are expertly framed
to allow for safe storage the rest of the year. Alternatively you
could consider making them into wall-hangings following the
general advice and instructions for the advent calendar on
page 66. To store these for next year, roll them up carefully and
pop them in a pillowcase or wrap with acid-free tissue paper.

Suppliers

DMC (UK)
DMC Creative World
Pullman Road, Wigston, Leicester, LE18 2DY
Tel: 01162 811040
Website: www.dmc.com

DMC (Australia)
DMC Needlecraft Pty Ltd.
51–66 Carrington Road, Marrickville, NSW 2204
Tel: 02 599 3088
Website: www.dmc.com

DMC (New Zealand)
Warnaar Trading Co Ltd.
376 Ferry Road, PO Box 19567, Christchurch
Tel: 03 89288
Website: www.dmc.com

Anchor (UK)
Coats Crafts UK
PO Box 22, Lingfield House, Lingfield Point,
McMullen Road, Darlington, Co Durham DL1 1YQ
Tel: + 1325 394237; Fax: + 1325 394200
Website: www.coatscrafts.co.uk

Anchor (USA)
Coats and Clark
PO Box 12229, Greenville, SC 29612-0229
Tel: (800) 648 1479
Website: www.coatsandclark.com

Panduro Hobby
Westway House, Transport Avenue
Brentford, Middlesex TW8 9HF, UK
Tel: 020 8847 6161; Fax: 020 8847 5073
Website: www.panduro.co.uk

Willow Fabrics
85 Town Lane, Mobberley
Knutsford, Cheshire WA16 7HH, UK
Tel: 0800 567 811; Fax: (01565) 872 239
Website: www.willowfabrics.com

Hobbycraft
Stores nationwide in the UK.
Website: www.hobbycraft.co.uk

Framecraft Miniatures Ltd
Lichfield Road, Brownhills
Walsall WS8 6LH, UK
Tel: (01543) 360 842; Fax: (01543) 453 154
Website: www.framecraft.com

Acknowledgments

All the usual suspects played their part in helping me produce this third design collection. So my love and thanks go to Ade my husband for just being there, my mam and dad who provided their usual support system together with Andrew and Sarah who ensured I had plenty of cuddles from gorgeous grandson Sam.

My thanks go to everyone at David & Charles for their technical expertise and continuing support for my work, and to Betsy Hosegood for her skilful editing. I can only express my amazement at the persuasive powers of Cheryl Brown who convinced me it was possible to write a book in less than a year. Despite my early misgivings I'm pleased to say that she was right and once again I'm indebted to her for her constant encouragement and enthusiasm for my designs. Lin Clements spent many painstaking hours converting my charts into little works of art and making my job much easier in the process. Daphne White and Jennifer Williams have stitched cheerfully and skilfully for me, somehow managing to juggle their family commitments with my deadlines. As usual, Pat Henson did a fantastic job on framing my designs while Cara Ackerman at DMC supplied me with beautiful threads and fabrics to keep me inspired. Without the continuing love, friendship and generosity of these people this book would never have been possible.

About the Author

Sue Cook has been a freelance designer since 1992 and in that time she has worked for all the major UK stitching magazines and created hundreds of Christmas designs. This will be Sue's fourth book and the third in her 'Collection' series with David & Charles. Sue lives in Newport, South Wales, with her husband Ade and their two Westies, Anna and Dylan.

DMC/Anchor Conversion Table

The designs in this book use DMC stranded cotton (floss). This DMC/Anchor thread conversion chart is only a guide, as exact colour comparisons cannot always be made. An asterisk * indicates an Anchor shade that has been used more than once so take care to avoid duplication in a design. If you wish to use Madeira threads, telephone for a conversion chart on 01765 640003 or email: acts@madeira.co.uk

DMC	Anchor	DMC	Anchor	DMC	Anchor	DMC	Anchor	DMC	Anchor	DMC	Anchor	DMC	Anchor	DMC	Anchor
B 5200	1	355	1014	604	55	781	308*	912	209	3023	899	3765	170	3846	1090
White	2	356	1013*	605	1094	782	308*	913	204	3024	388*	3766	167	3847	1076*
Ecru	387*	367	216	606	334	783	307	915	1029	3031	905*	3768	779	3848	1074*
150	59	368	214	608	330*	791	178	917	89	3032	898*	3770	1009	3849	1070*
151	73	369	1043	610	889	792	941	918	341	3033	387*	3772	1007	3850	188*
152	969	370	888*	611	898*	793	176*	919	340	3041	871	3773	1008	3851	186*
153	95*	371	887*	612	832	794	175	920	1004	3042	870	3774	778	3852	306*
154	873	372	887*	613	831	796	133	921	1003*	3045	888*	3776	1048*	3853	1003*
155	1030*	400	351	632	936	797	132	922	1003*	3046	887*	3777	1015	3854	313
156	118*	402	1047*	640	393	798	146	924	851	3047	887	3778	1013*	3855	311*
157	120*	407	914	642	392	799	145	926	850	3051	845*	3779	868	3856	347
158	178	413	236*	644	391	800	144	927	849	3052	844	3781	1050	3857	936*
159	120*	414	235*	645	273	801	359	928	274	3053	843	3782	388*	3858	1007
160	175*	415	398	646	8581*	806	169	930	1035	3064	883	3787	904*	3859	914*
161	176	420	374	647	1040	807	168	931	1034	3072	397	3790	904*	3860	379*
162	159*	422	372	648	900	809	130	932	1033	3078	292	3799	236*	3861	378
163	877	433	358	666	46	813	161*	934	852*	3325	129	3801	1098	3862	358*
164	240*	434	310	676	891	814	45	935	861	3326	36	3802	1019*	3863	379*
165	278*	435	365	677	361*	815	44	936	846	3328	1024	3803	69	3864	376
166	280*	436	363	680	901*	816	43	937	268*	3340	329	3804	63*	3865	2*
167	375*	437	362	699	923*	817	13*	938	381	3341	328	3805	62*	3866	926*
168	274*	444	291	700	228	818	23*	939	152*	3345	268*	3806	62*	48	1207
169	849*	445	288	701	227	819	271	943	189	3346	267*	3807	122	51	1220*
208	110	451	233	702	226	820	134	945	881	3347	266*	3808	1068	52	1209*
209	109	452	232	703	238	822	390	946	332	3348	264	3809	1066*	57	1203*
210	108	453	231	704	256*	823	152*	947	330*	3350	77	3810	1066*	61	1218*
211	342	469	267*	712	926	824	164	948	1011	3354	74	3811	1060	62	1202*
221	897*	470	266*	718	88	825	162*	950	4146	3362	263	3812	188	67	1212
223	895	471	265	720	326	826	161*	951	1010	3363	262	3813	875*	69	1218*
224	895	472	253	721	324	827	160	954	203*	3364	261	3814	1074	75	1206*
225	1026	498	1005	722	323*	828	9159	955	203*	3371	382	3815	877*	90	1217*
300	352	500	683	725	305*	829	906	956	40*	3607	87	3816	876*	91	1211
301	1049*	501	878	726	295*	830	277*	957	50	3608	86	3817	875*	92	1215*
304	19	502	877*	727	293	831	277*	958	187	3609	85	3818	923*	93	1210*
307	289	503	876*	729	890	832	907*	959	186	3685	1028	3819	278	94	1216
309	42	504	206*	730	845*	833	874*	961	76*	3687	68	3820	306	95	1209*
310	403	517	162*	731	281*	834	874*	962	75*	3688	75*	3821	305*	99	1204
311	148	518	1039	732	281*	838	1088	963	23*	3689	49	3822	295*	101	1213*
312	979	519	1038	733	280	839	1086	964	185	3705	35*	3823	386	102	1209*
315	1019*	520	862*	734	279	840	1084	966	240	3706	33*	3824	8*	103	1210*
316	1017	522	860	738	361*	841	1082	970	925	3708	31	3825	323*	104	1217*
317	400	523	859	739	366	842	1080	971	316*	3712	1023	3826	1049*	105	1218*
318	235*	524	858	740	316*	844	1041	972	298	3713	1020	3827	311	106	1203*
319	1044*	535	401	741	304	869	375	973	290	3716	25	3828	373	107	1203*
320	215	543	933	742	303	890	218	975	357	3721	896	3829	901*	108	1220*
321	47	550	101*	743	302	891	35*	976	1001	3722	1027	3830	5975	111	1218*
322	978	552	99	744	301	892	33*	977	1002	3726	1018	3831	29	112	1201*
326	59*	553	98	745	300	893	27	986	246	3727	1016	3832	28	113	1210*
327	101*	554	95	746	275	894	26	987	244	3731	76*	3833	31*	114	1213*
333	119	561	212	747	158	895	1044*	988	243	3733	75*	3834	100*	115	1206*
334	977	562	210	754	1012	898	380	989	242	3740	872	3835	98*	121	1210*
335	40*	563	208	758	9575	899	38	991	1076	3743	869	3836	90	122	1215*
336	150	564	206*	760	1022	900	333	992	1072	3746	1030	3837	100*	124	1210*
340	118	580	924	761	1021	902	897*	993	1070	3747	120	3838	177	125	1213*
341	117*	581	281*	762	234	904	258	995	410	3750	1036	3839	176*	126	1209*
347	1025	597	1064	772	259*	905	257	996	433	3752	1032	3840	120*		
349	13*	598	1062	775	128	906	256*	3011	856	3753	1031	3841	159*		
350	11	600	59*	776	24	907	255	3012	855	3755	140	3842	164*		
351	10	601	63*	778	968	909	923*	3013	853	3756	1037	3843	1089*		
352	9	602	57	779	380*	910	230	3021	905*	3760	162*	3844	410*		
353	8*	603	62*	780	309	911	205	3022	8581*	3761	928	3845	1089*		

Index